PONTIUS
PILATE

STUDIES IN RELIGION AND CULTURE

Frank Burch Brown, Gary L. Ebersole, and Edith Wyschogrod, Editors

ROGER CAILLOIS

PONTIUS PILATE

Translated by Charles Lam Markmann

Introduction by Ivan Strenski

University of Virginia Press
Charlottesville

University of Virginia Press
Originally published in French as *Ponce Pilate*, © Éditions Gallimard,
Paris, 1961
Introduction © 2006 by the Rector and Visitors of the
University of Virginia
Printed in the United States of America on acid-free paper

First University of Virginia Press edition published 2006

9 8 7 6 5 4 3 2 1

Library of Congress Cataloging-in-Publication Data
Caillois, Roger, 1913–
    Pontius pilate / Roger Caillois ; translated by Charles Lam Mark-
mann ; introduction by Ivan Strenski.
        p.   cm. — (Studies in religion and culture)
    ISBN 0-8139-2551-7 (cloth : alk. paper)
    1. Pilate, Pontius, 1st cent.—Fiction. I. Markmann, Charles Lam. II.
Title. III. Studies in religion and culture (Charlottesville, Va.)
    PQ2663.A38P66   2006
    843'.914—dc22

                                                    2005028876

CONTENTS

Introduction

At Play in the Mind of Pilate

Ivan Strenski

A World of "What Ifs"

The Gospels are peopled with characters who march
onstage only to stray from the set or get whisked off
without trace. Scripture teases us with countless "what
ifs." The Bible seems not even curious about the fate
of its lost characters—even when they played poten-
tially key roles in the Gospel story or could have made
a difference to its outcome. What became of the high
priest's servant after his severed ear had been miraculously restored? Is there any doubt that he must have
turned to Jesus? And, if so, might he not have played a
pivotal role as living proof of Jesus's divinity, sufficient
perhaps to head off his crucifixion? What if Lazarus,
recently resurrected by Jesus, had been employed for
the same purpose? How could their combined testimony have been gainsaid? Of course, events might
have taken another course, as indeed they seem to have
done. What if, instead of backing up Jesus's claims
to divinity when he most needed them, they had re-

mained mute? About such possible "what ifs" the Gospels just do not care. But some of us do care.

How else to explain the rave popularity of Dan Brown's *Da Vinci Code*—a whole volume constructed to satisfy the appetites for an elaborately devised scheme of "what ifs"? The Gospels certainly give us license to think more about Jesus and Magdalene than meets the eye. So they leave it to a modern novelist to open a franchise for curiosity about the possibilities inherent in this tantalizing situation. What if that womanly creature seated to the right of Jesus in Leonardo's *Last Supper* is Mary Magdalene? And if Leonardo knows enough to place "her" there, just what does he know? Of course, about these possibilities and others the canonical Gospels do not—or will not—speak. Small wonder so many religious imaginations have shifted into an overdrive of speculation about such scriptural puzzles.

This is to point out that while the official Gospels care little about many of their more consequential characters, such as Lazarus, Magdalene, and others, the purveyors of "sacred fantasy fiction" care a great deal. Case in point again, Brown's *Da Vinci Code* calls some of the Gospels' more intriguing but vagrant characters, like Magdalene, back onto the set. This restaging of the drama of salvation in Brown's hands becomes his tale of sacred fantasy, fleshing out the "what ifs" surrounding Jesus and Magdalene to reveal a bright bloodline of their union leading right up to our own time. Beyond potboilers like Brown's *Da Vinci Code*, even heftier works of sacred fiction like Nikos Kazantzakis's *Last Temptation of Christ*—together with Martin Scorsese's film version of the novel—do much the same thing. They pick up a "what if" and run with it. In Scorsese's film, what if—as would be natural—the resurrected Lazarus became a local celebrity, not to mention a major curiosity? The Bible does not report this. But how could Lazarus not be what Scorsese imagines? Running with this "what if," Scorsese fantasizes a Lazarus more dazed than lucid, still flummoxed by his resurrection. What if Lazarus were queried about those four lost days of life? Not satisfied with spinning out the "what ifs" of the Lazarus story this far, Scorsese concludes by poking a finger in our eyes: Lazarus gives a shrug and confesses to his thrill-seeking inquisitors that the afterlife was not, after all, that different from the earthly one! What are we to think of that? The official Gospels do not—or will not—even raise the subject. But sacred fantasists revel in such possibilities.

The novel before us, *Pontius Pilate*, written by one of France's great men of letters of the twentieth century, Roger Caillois (1913–78), takes its place alongside the "sacred fantasies" of Brown, Kazantzakis,

Scorsese, and others. In a little over a hundred rapid pages, divided into seven short chapters, Caillois conjures visions of countless plausible dramas of "what if" played out inside the procurator's mind during the final twenty-four hours before he decides the fate of Jesus. What if his decision were less one of a soulless bureaucrat and more one of a conflicted fellow human being? Caillois' novella ponders the mysteries of this climactic part of the biblical narrative.

Constructed as a series of interviews arranged to help Pilate decide the fate of Jesus, each chapter dramatizes the particular perspectives that might have faced the procurator. The riveting exchanges with Judas play upon the ironies of Jesus's ineluctable death. Is not the betrayal of Jesus, as Caillois' Judas claims, a necessary sacrifice in aid of cosmic salvation? How else, Caillois in effect suggests, to relate the conversations between Pilate, the contemptuous cosmopolite, and his fierce provincial opponents, the Jewish priests Annas and Caiaphas, than as paradigms of cagey diplomatic maneuvering? Finally, could Pilate's interrogation of Jesus the God-man have been anything but the bizarre collision of irreconcilable worlds that Caillois makes of it?

Caillois' fascination with the mix of religion and politics dominates these initial four chapters. Pilate debates "church and state" with the Jewish leadership.

Menenius

He queries the amoral counsel of his savvy Roman political advisor, Menenius, to ignore Jewish religious scruples entirely. Pilate vainly deploys the logic of secular rationalism to cool the apocalyptic ravings of Judas, revealed here as a frothing epileptic seer. A stone-silent Jesus reduces Pilate to utter frustration, making him, in effect, answer his own questions. Sacred and profane are left in a standoff.

Juxtaposed to this tedious day of official disputations recorded in these first four chapters, Pilate finds blessed relief in the fifth chapter's account of a lush evening of feasting and drinking, entertained by the electrifying conversation of the only Jew that Pilate respects enough to have become his personal confidant, the mercurial Mardouk. As if possessed by some visionary spirit, Mardouk lays before Pilate the many diverging but unavoidable events that will flood into history following each possible decision he might make. Thus the early mood of relaxation gives way to even deeper introspection as Pilate falls under the spell of Mardouk's intellectual sorcery. In the final two chapters, Pilate struggles through a sleepless night of indecision, sorting through the day's discordant voices in what must have been for him the longest night of his life. Caillois closes with the most enigmatic of epilogues.

Of all these dialogues, none is more revealing about

Mardouk

Stoicism —

the character of Pilate than the discussions with his Roman counselor, Menenius. This Machiavelli lays out a strategy of expedience that would allow Pilate to finesse political control over a Judea that seems to be gradually slipping from his grasp. Menenius counsels the release of Barrabas and an ostentatious washing of hands as deliberate acts of political stagecraft. Let this one man die for the sake of the good order maintained thereby for the many, Menenius coolly advises. But even as Pilate's prudence responds to Menenius's political calculus, both made yet sounder by their fit with Roman imperial *réal politique*, that smaller—inner— voice of Pilate's conscience strains to be heard. The procurator is touched, if only slightly, by an equally Roman ideal of Stoic justice that is also part of who he is. This prospect of an inner struggle for Pilate's soul, no matter how unfair the fight, is one of the best reasons for bothering to think about him at all. In Pilate's agonies over difficult choices, Caillois makes the procurator painfully human. Pilate understands the transcendent demands of his personal code of Stoic justice. Yet in terms of really living up to its lofty standards, he can manage only a wish.

So Pilate's ultimate truth is the depth of his own cowardice—or at best his confrontation of it. Perhaps seeing in him our own string of life's petty, and not so petty, defeats, we "know" how at least *his* story will end. Or do we? At times, the forces arrayed against Pilate can seem insurmountable. Worse yet, his character flaws, so keenly obvious to him, are even more transparent and brilliantly targeted by his energetic religious and political opponents. Judas fears that Pilate's mediocrity has such a thorough and complete hold on his nature that even it cannot be trusted to carry the day! Annas and Caiaphas see so well into the soft center of Pilate's soul that they feel no need to "plunge in their knives." It is enough for them to flash them unsheathed before him. Why is it that our enemies can sometimes know us even better than we know ourselves? Pilate has such enemies, and they will not relent.

This edition of Caillois' *Pontius Pilate*, then, seeks to make available once again for the English-reading public some of the most engaging and unsettling thinking in print about what may have played in the mind of Pilate as he moved toward sentencing Jesus to death. To Caillois, the dilemmas facing Pilate all offer possible choices along which many potential futures can be plotted. We know how Pilate faced constraints to the exercise of imperial Roman power in the face of the religious zeal of an unruly local population. But what if other choices had been as real and as available? The drama of Pilate's situation, as Caillois constructs it, is his being poised amidst impossibly bad options, any of which Pilate might have chosen. To condemn Jesus, whom he believes to be the innocent victim of religious fanaticism, would dishonor his sense of Roman justice and concede moral territory to fanatics. But to release Jesus would invite popular uprising in Judea and dash his careerist hopes of escape from this provincial backwater for the salons of the metropole. Caillois helps us understand what an honorable, or alternately shrewd, man might do with such options.

In the case of Pilate, we have little to go on in divining his inner thoughts. Only Matthew 27:19 offers brief glimpses into Pilate's private self. The sleep of his wife, Procula, had been upset by dreams warning against Pilate's taking part in condemning Jesus. What if Pilate had taken Procula's trusted advice? On the one hand, she spoke to Pilate's conscience; on the other hand, the threat of public outcry reminded Pilate of how weak was his hold on public order in Judea. Does a man so constrained have no actual choices? Caillois argues that he does. But unlike Caillois, the canonical Gospels do not—or will not—chart Pilate's way through these crosscurrents of "what ifs" as he seeks resolution to his dilemmas. The Gospels leave us instead with puzzles they themselves do not even address.

Fundamental to all fantastic sacred fiction such as *Pontius Pilate* is the desire to stir the religious imagination into creative thinking. What if Kazantzakis and Scorsese are right that Jesus had to grow gradually into a realization of his divinity? What if Jesus were less a prepackaged being who was always conscious of his mission and its realization? What if Jesus were more like a God who was also fully a man, as Kazantzakis and Scorsese seek to portray him? How would this change the view that Christians had of Christianity, and of their own struggles to live loyally by the will of God? If Kazantzakis were right, Christians would be more Christlike in sharing with Jesus a gradually revealed discovery of what God intends for them. What if "Christ's nature . . . was profoundly human," asks Kazantzakis, and thus what if Jesus were racked with doubts about his own identity and divine mission—much as we are by our own role in God's plan? What if, as Kazantzakis shows in depicting this struggling, searching Jesus, Christ had "within him this warm human element?" For Kazantzakis, the conclusion is clear: without his profound humanity, Christ "would never be able to touch our hearts with such assurance and tenderness; he would not be able to become a model for our lives" (Kazantzakis, 3). The only way that such expansive religious meditations on the nature of Jesus might warm the hearts of the faithful would be if they went along with the likes of "blasphemers" Kazantzakis and Scorsese and willingly suspended both belief and disbelief to enter the imaginal religious worlds of novel and film. Caillois invites us—believers and skeptics alike—to do the same with Pilate as his better-known fellow travelers have done with Jesus.

What the Bible Will Not Say and Caillois Will

While Caillois may mirror the modern religious imagination of a Kazantzakis or a Scorsese, what may catch today's reader unawares is the way Caillois echoes the "what if" style of some of Christianity's oldest documents. At least two noncanonical Gospels speculate on Pilate and on the mysteries of his momentous decision: the Gospel of Peter and the Acts of Pilate, or Gospel of Nicodemus (hereafter abbreviated AP). It ought to be noted straightaway that behind their entertaining of "what ifs" about Pilate is a problematic early Christian anti-Judaism. "What if" the Jews are entirely responsible for the fate of Jesus and Pilate is mostly innocent, these "Gospels" argue. Caillois, as we will see, has far different reasons for entertaining the "what ifs" of Pilate. But common to both efforts is the imaginative recasting of Pilate's role in the story of the death of Jesus.

In the Acts of Pilate, for example, the procurator is cast much as Caillois conceives of him—as if he were reluctant to yield to the bloodthirsty call for

Jesus's crucifixion because of his high Roman ethical standards, something absent from biblical testimony. In the Acts of Pilate, the procurator rebuffs the pressures applied by Annas and Caiaphas not once or twice as the New Testament testifies but again and again, yielding only when all resistance fails. When Pilate demands reasons for Jesus's execution, Jesus's accusers cite his transgressions of sacred law by healing on the Sabbath. Stunned, Pilate replies with withering sarcasm: "For a good work do they desire to put him to death?" (AP 2:6). Or when Jesus is first brought to him, Pilate instructs his troops to bring Jesus "hither, but with gentleness"—a far cry from the canonical Pilate's bureaucratic command to have Jesus scourged within an inch of his life (AP 1:6). The Acts of Pilate even concocts a scene of Pilate trying vainly to "make nice" with Jesus's Jewish accusers by noting that his wife, Procula, had recently converted to Judaism (AP 2:1). Incidentally, it is not only the Acts of Pilate that imagines that this might be true, since the tradition of Procula's conversion to Judaism is maintained by the Coptic church. Moreover, Procula's subsequent recognition of Jesus as Messiah promoted her to sainthood in the Coptic church. Finally, in a bizarre coup of invention, the Acts of Pilate casts Jesus actively recruiting Pilate to play his part in realizing the scripted drama of his passion and death. Jesus directs Pilate, in

effect, to get on with it and set the stage for his crucifixion: "And the procurator ordered the Jews to go
outside of the praetorium; and summoning Jesus, he
says to Him: 'What shall I do to thee?' Jesus says to
Pilate: 'As it has been given to thee.' Pilate says: 'How
given?' Jesus says: 'Moses and the prophets have proclaimed beforehand of my death and resurrection'"
(AP 4:3). Thus in a time when it was regarded as more
pious to give freer rein to the religious imagination,
however unsavory its polemic, than in our own days of
scriptural sclerosis, those unruly early Christians bris-
tled at limits on their thinking about Pilate, Jesus, or
other actors in the drama of salvation.

Between Radical Religion and Real Politics

If early Christian anti-Judaism lies behind the "what
ifs" of these apocryphal "Gospels," what drives Caillois' imaginative retelling of the story of Pontius Pilate? While there may be no definite answer, much
of Caillois' novella reverberates loudly with his own
time. In parading the possibilities that pass by Pilate,
Caillois conjures up a world caught in raging religious
and political turmoil. As a Roman bureaucrat, Pilate
represents mundane order and the rule of human laws
among a people craving the transcendent ecstasies of
self-immolation. Caillois' own times resonate with this
same theme. His novella was written at the height of

the Algerian War, which some interpreters have seen as a conflict between an "enlightened," albeit imperialist, republican France and a partly fundamentalist Muslim rebellion in Algeria. Can this struggle be seen playing in the background of Caillois' own mind, generating, in its turn, a whole series of "what ifs"? Both Caillois and history record the conflict of Pilate's universalist rational principles of justice over against Jewish religious zealots contemptuous of such abstractions and, moreover, impatient to die for their beliefs. Caillois puts us into the thoughts of a Pilate besieged on all sides by political and religious pressures he would rather ignore. His fitful record of resisting such forces does not inspire confidence. One such recent occasion found Pilate woefully wanting. A Jewish demonstration against his imposition of the symbols of Roman authority threatened to turn violent. Pilate might have dispersed the gathering with a routine show of military force. But the Jewish insurrectionists were not intimidated by mundane power. Instead, flaunting their contempt for all things worldly, the Jewish demonstrators literally threw themselves before the sword. Pilate backed down. Of Caillois' Pilate, Yeats's words ring true: "the best lack all conviction while the worst are full of passionate intensity."

In terms of the religious fundamentalism of our own time, what if Pilate regarded the religious zeal of the Jews in the same way as Caillois may have considered the rebel Muslims of Algeria? What rational tactics and strategies might dissuade an enemy who does not reckon loss of life—an enemy bent on waging a religious war, stocked with the weapons of martyrdom and suicide bombing?

Generous readers will grant that the politically informed Caillois might have had such historical parallels in mind as he composed *Pontius Pilate* in the late 1950s: the analogy of Pilate's struggles with Jewish religious nationalism in ancient Palestine to France's agonies over Islamic nationalism in Algeria. Caillois' meditation on the vexing nature of this struggle, with all that it implied about the potency of religious factors in contemporary international affairs, indeed anticipates our "civilizational" politics.

It becomes more persuasive to consider an Algerian War subtext given that the date of the original publication of Caillois' *Pontius Pilate* (1961) coincided with the near civil war brought about in France by President Charles de Gaulle's decision to abandon Algeria to the rebels. Worse still in the minds of the anti-Gaullist "Ultras" than yielding to the Algerian independence forces was their president's decision to invade Algeria to quell the revolt of his fellow countrymen. Burned into the minds of the French "Ultras" was their acute sense of betrayal at the hands of de Gaulle. In like

man in the middle.
principle between extremes and
expediency

manner, Caillois dwells on similar sources of Pilate's
sense of humiliation. Pilate's deep feelings of shame,
however, come not only from his cowardice before religious fanaticism; he was also deeply chagrined by the
craven eagerness of his superiors in Rome to concili-
ate the Jews. This undermining of the historical Pilate
proved so effective that an envious fellow provincial
Roman military consul, Vitellius, successfully plotted *Vitellius*
in Syria to bring about the procurator's fall and his
own swift succession to Pilate's office. Vitellius's ma-
neuver ultimately achieved Pilate's undoing in 36 CE.

Since the 1960s, it has been liberationist fashion to
cast the Algerian War in terms of a nascent postcolonial discourse. For this constituency, the Algerian War
was really about a paradigmatic struggle for colonial
self-determination, a feat of mytho-political heroism
by the wretched of the earth. But politico-religious
developments of our own time have given some con-
trarian intellectuals pause to reflect upon the certainties of earlier *tiers-mondiste* enthusiasms. What indeed
was the Algerian struggle really about, given the dismal record of the new nation in the interval? Why, if
political independence be such a boon, have so many
Algerian intellectuals taken refuge in the old colonial
capital? What, too, are we to make of the dismal politics of the place—the disenchanting lurches between
military dictatorship and corrupt civilian rule, finally

taking the form of an inglorious impasse between military government and Islamist radicals?

No less a figure than the "New Philosopher" Bernard-Henri Lévy figures prominently among those who question the certainties of postcolonial liberationist discourse. The struggle between a modernizing but self-doubting cosmopolitanism and a religiously self-assured but fiercely intolerant provincialism continues apace. Even independence has not put an end to this. Anthropologist and later governor general of Algeria Jacques Soustelle saw France's mission in Algeria as nothing less than an extension of the French Revolution's liberation of peoples from religion. By maintaining a "French" Algeria, these advocates of universal human freedom believed that they could rescue Algeria's Muslims from their own local "superstitions"—a cramped, inward-looking Algerian Islam! Says Soustelle, in arguing for "French" Algeria: "We would be errant swine were we to abandon to their own destiny people who count on us to liberate them from their ancestral and religious dependency; they are half-way there by their own efforts and are on the road to democracy. Can we now, have the right to abandon them in that half-way state?" (Lévy, 286). Georges Bidault, the Resistance fighter and an early minister in de Gaulle's first government after liberation from the Nazis, sounded a similar note half a century ago:

A choice has to be made; either we believe in the inequality of the races, [and] we consider that democracy, the Rights of Man, and parliamentary government are acceptable on one side of the Mediterranean but not on the other—and I would then understand if we decided to abandon the Algerians; or we are humanists, universalists to the end, and we consider that parliamentary democracy, the generalised right of habeas corpus, and the rule of law are preferable for the Algerians as well. In those circumstances, our sole duty and Republican obligation is to treat the Algerian people as the people and language of Brittany were treated a century ago. (Lévy, 287)

Likewise, in this fanciful tale, Caillois depicts the events leading up to the trial of Jesus from the point of view of Pontius Pilate, seen as a rational colonial administrator of an earlier era, likewise stuck in a Middle Eastern dependency convulsed with religious fundamentalism. Like the French idealists with their universalist ambitions for Algeria, Pilate too was once inspired by the high-minded idealistic purpose of bringing both Bidault's rule of law and Soustelle's freedom from religious "superstition" to Palestine. To some extent this novella can be understood as an allegory of these cultural clashes, framed within tan-

talizing "what ifs." Caillois' narrative should therefore interest not only literary critics and theorists but
also religious studies scholars, political scientists, and
indeed all those who care about the witches' brew of
politics and religion that bubbles away to widespread
dismay.

Pilate in Fact and Ficcione

If perennial, and specifically French, struggles with
nationalist religious zealotry lurk in the background of
Caillois' novella, there is equally well a literary background that helps us understand his project. The great
Argentine fantasist Jorge Luis Borges, and his con-
ception of a *ficcione*, stand behind Caillois' *Pontius Pilate*. Here indeed seems the source of that persistent
posing of "what ifs" that sets the tone of the novella.
In 1939, Caillois fled occupied France for Argentina,
both to escape the Nazis and to resume his liaison
with the brilliant Argentine essayist and founder of the
avant-garde Buenos Aires literary journal *Sur*, Victo-
ria Ocampo. Through Ocampo, Caillois fell in with a
circle of Argentine literati and philosophers cluster-
ing around Borges. Caillois' devotion to the Argentine master was instant, and he became one of Borges's
closer literary companions, promoting Borges's reputation in Europe. Caillois was single-handedly responsible for introducing Borges to the Francophone read-

ing audience through some of the first translations of his works into French. By the time Caillois returned to liberated France, he was thoroughly imbued with the spirit of Borges's literary genius and an active coworker alongside him in advancing the prestige of the literary forms for which Borges gained his well-deserved worldwide reputation.

Chief among the genres applying to *Pontius Pilate* is what Borges has called "*ficciones*." These "fictions" Borges refers to as "notes on *imaginary* books," "tales of fantasy" delighting in the "unreality" of purportedly actual historical events, persons, and places (Borges, 67). Borges literally creates what appear to be real books out of the "thin air" of his imaginings. What marks them, however, is that he infuses fantasy with the heavier air of verisimilitude. He loads his fanciful imaginings with encyclopedic levels of concrete, precise, and indubitable facts. This flood of facts then swamps the suspicions of the conventional reader into presuming a wholesale correspondence with historical reality. *Pontius Pilate* is such a Borgesian "fiction."

Pontius Pilate even takes a further step beyond Borgesian *ficciones* by including an exhilarating *ficcione* within a *ficcione* in a chapter on the "prophecies" that flow from the mouth of Pilate's Jewish confrere, Mardouk. There Mardouk forecasts (or does he merely concoct?) a scenario of concrete prospective historical *when truth is stranger than fiction, the good storyteller opts for the fiction. And so it is with some of the stories surround Jesus. I may not know all of the story, but I know more than most*

happenings variously unsettling to our conventional religious expectations. In one of his wild half-fanciful, half-clairvoyant visions into the future, Mardouk's mind gushes forth in a flood of counterfactual "what ifs," all turning on the likely outcomes of each of Pilate's possible decisions about the fate of Jesus. If Pilate should act one way, Mardouk "sees" (or does he "create"?) a future in which Pilate and his wife become saints in the Ethiopian Church—as indeed we know they came to be. If Pilate acts otherwise, other equally plausible (or implausible) concrete consequences follow. Caillois soon loses us in a dizzying confusion of truths and "fictions."

A Sacred "Fiction" of Transgression

Finally, in a book with such explicit religious bearing, one cannot ignore Caillois' long-standing involvement in the discourse of the sacred. Caillois is well practiced in theorizing the eruption of the sacred into politics, as witnessed by his own little masterpiece, *Man and the Sacred* (1939). There he tells us that the sacred dances to its own logic, typically out of step with our tidy conventions of thought and action. Accordingly, Caillois' Pilate is painfully aware of the difficulty (impossibility?) of administering a polity overheated with religious passion. The seduction of apocalyptic visions, the fascination with mysteries resisting ordinary

sacred dances to its own logic

understanding, all bedevil the attempts by the procurators of this world to control them. The sacred, no matter how attractive, is deadly dangerous. Like Moses before the burning bush, God's white-hot light drew the patriarch toward it, yet it also filled him with dread at his approach to God's limitless power. Caillois, too, knows how simultaneously seductive and destructive the power of religion can be, especially in the political form we find here in *Pontius Pilate*. We have to take care not to get burned, as the volatile mix of religion and politics in today's world shows us. Whether this takes the form of Osama bin Laden's brand of radical Islam, or James Dobson's radical Christian campaign against gay marriage, or even Martin Luther King Jr.'s nonviolent revolution for civil rights, when religion and politics mix, the resulting compound can inflame attitudes and ignite passions like nothing else.

Caillois grew to intellectual maturity in the Paris of the 1920s and 1930s in a milieu well attuned by the rise of fascism to the notion of just such a "sacred" politics. Indeed, in his early years, Caillois seemed to have welcomed precisely the kind of transvaluation of values in the Nietzschean air of his milieu, especially as given shape by his longtime friend and associate Georges Bataille. One-time collaborators in the Collège de Sociologie and the surrealist movements of the late 1930s, Bataille and Caillois were at the center of a good deal of radical interwar intellectual excitement. But Caillois' alliance with Bataille would not last.

A radical Nietzschean, Bataille authored perverse theories of the sacred as a transgressive assault on all that was sacred in the conventional sense. In Bataille's view, this sacred had become nigh unto profane because of its relentless domestication at the trivializing hands of bourgeois society. Bataille's solution to radical profanation was to revive human sacrifice as an exemplary rite. The violent otherness of the human immolations that he had envisioned would shake modern folk out of their smug secularity by being performed as a public spectacle in the center of Paris. In this effort Bataille proved himself a force of savage imagination that could not be conciliated with the gentler virtues of Caillois' late-blooming humanism. Caillois broke with Bataille over his old comrade's plan.

In the 1930s, Caillois also saw more clearly than Bataille how fascism actualized a program of an extreme transgressive sacred politics. This gave Caillois added incentive to turn his back on Bataille's extremism, developing in its stead a posthumanist humanism evident in the compassion and the sense of justice of so unlikely a character as Pilate. This transgressive sacred stirring of the mundane political world is one of the things that *Pontius Pilate* holds up to critical light.

One consequence of Caillois' estrangement from Bataille's ideal of a perverse and transgressive sacred was Caillois' adoption of a kindly and playful humanism that focused all his work to the very end. Significantly, the one-time surrealist devoted his latter days not to mounting violent spectacles of transgression but rather to serving the cultural and educational mission of the United Nations at UNESCO (1948) and then later, from 1952 until his death in 1978, as the founder and first editor of the international interdisciplinary journal *Diogenes*. As a tribute to his eclectic and fertile literary production of some forty years, Caillois was elected to the Académie française in 1971. He was received there in phrases well in keeping with the spirit of his life's work: "You are, dear sir, one of the most inquisitive minds of our times, one of its most independent, yet, you are one of the most resistant to its blandishments." Even while seated comfortably in his place in the Institute, Caillois lived up to this reputation for independence and playfulness. One observer noted that in those grave deliberations by the members of the Académie over the legitimacy of certain words entering French usage, Caillois would sometimes propose the *ficciones* of nonexistent dictionary entries complete with supporting, but bogus, etymologies. It was in the midst of those postwar years of

Caillois' ripening—and sly—humanism that his *Ponce Pilate* was published in 1961 and translated into English the following year.

In *Pontius Pilate*, as Caillois' reception into the Académie française suggests, the author can give voice to surrealism's irritation with bourgeois cultural discourse yet without Bataille's snarl and bite. Caillois well recognizes that Pilate's once elegant "What is truth?" or his dramatic "washing of hands" barely ripples the surface of conventional consciousness. To break through such clichés, Caillois creates fanciful background stories that deepen our sense of what these mysteries mean. Pilate's reference to "truth" indicates an unrecognized philosophic turn of mind, so out of character with the career military. But just whom did Pilate think he was fooling with the shabby political stunt of washing his hands? If we take seriously Pilate's philosophic sophistication, as Caillois would have us do, how could Pilate have believed he was free of responsibility thanks to this trite piece of street theater? Caillois fantasizes an entire background story accounting for how this could be by taking us deep behind the scenes of the Pilate of the Gospels into the depths of his fertile imagination.

In the pages to follow, readers will discover a work both serious and entertaining. They will experience the thrill of intellectual fireworks and spiritual quests but also the delight of wicked ironies by a droll master storyteller. Keep an open mind. This *ficcione*, this simulacrum of historical truth, has been served up for you. Enjoy the strange delights of entering a stranger world still, where the unexpected and the expected contend as equals on a level field of play.

Bibliography

Borges, Jorge Luis. "Foreword: The Garden of Forking Paths." *In Jorge Luis Borges: Collected Fictions*, edited by A. Hurley. New York: Penguin, 1998.

Caillois, Roger. *Man and the Sacred*. 1939. Translated by Meyer Barash. Champaign: University of Illinois Press, 2001.

Kazantzakis, Nikos. *The Last Temptation of Christ*. Translated by P. A. Bien. New York: Simon and Schuster, 1960.

Lévy, Bernard-Henri. "All Saints' Night: A Comment on the Possible Worthiness of the French Algerian Cause." In *Adventures along the Freedom Road: The French Intellectuals in the 20th Century*, edited by Bernard-Henri Lévy. London: Harvill, 1995.

PONTIUS
PILATE

ONE

The Priests

AT DAWN, PILATE WAS TOLD
OF THE ARREST OF JESUS
AND, ALMOST AT THE SAME
MOMENT, OF THE ARRIVAL
OF ANNAS AND CAIAPHAS, WHO
DEMANDED AN EMERGENCY
AUDIENCE, BUT OUTSIDE
THE PALACE, SINCE THEIR RELIGION
FORBADE THEM THE SLIGHTEST
CONTACT WITH IMPURITY
ON A HOLY DAY. PILATE, THOUGH
HE HAD SPENT SEVERAL
YEARS IN HIS POST, HAD NEVER
CEASED TO BE IRRITATED BY
SUCH AN ATTITUDE.
NONETHELESS,
HE HAD NO CHOICE BUT TO
YIELD TO IT. HIS MOST SERIOUS
PROBLEMS HAD ARISEN FROM
RESISTANCE TO SUCH FANATICISM
IN THE PEOPLE.

In the matter of the banners, he had had to give in. In the dispute over the aqueduct he had stood firm, but men had been wounded and killed. Latterly, when the Jews had insisted that he remove the shields bearing the name of Caesar from Herod's old palace where he had ordered them hung, he had fallen back on the power of inertia. The Jews had complained to Tiberius and the Emperor had overruled Pilate; with a bitter heart he had had to direct the removal of the hated emblems. That wound had not healed. He had sought to proclaim Caesar's sovereignty on the walls of his home, and Caesar, yielding to the protests of a conquered people instead of sustaining his own deputy, had made him remove from the walls not only his own name but the very symbol of Rome's power.

The orders from Rome were definitive: to respect local beliefs and customs as much as possible. In this Pilate saw a kind of unpardonable dereliction. Made wiser by recent experience, he was afraid that the incident of the night before would bring him yet another humiliation. In any case, he found it irritating, and it seemed grotesque to him that conquered men, even if they were priests, should be allowed to compel the Emperor's representative to treat with them anywhere other than in the rooms where he normally performed his duties. He was angry with himself for yielding to superstitious fantasies whose equivalent, in Rome, he would not hesitate to deride openly. This was not the contempt of the Roman for the Oriental, of the conqueror for the defeated; it was the revulsion of the philosopher against man's credulity. In Rome, nothing could prevent him from making fun of the augurs or smiling at the ancient prohibitions surrounding the priest of Jupiter.

In such circumstances, it galled him that in Jerusalem he could not treat the Jewish religion with the same disregard that in Rome he showed for the Roman faith. This political subservience angered him. And moreover, as the representative of Tiberius, he obviously embodied order, reason and law, justice and power. It pained him that the orders he received were so absurd that, in order to avoid clashes (which, however, could not be prevented from time to time), he had to stoop to hypocrisy. If Rome was the bearer of civilisation and peace, it was unworthy of her to bow for expediency's sake to every ridiculous custom. In that case, it were better to have remained behind her Seven Hills and never to have conquered Italy or the world.

Bitterly resigned, Pilate sent word to the emissaries of the Sanhedrin that he would go to them immediately. Then he asked for a report on the unsanctioned action of the day before, in which he found new grounds for vexation. From the beginning, he had distrusted that unled mob, armed with clubs and swords and guided by torches and lanterns, going by night without a warrant to seize a preacher who had not been formally accused. Had they perhaps wanted to confront him with an accomplished fact? worse still, if it were a matter of an unplanned outbreak, a spontaneous brawl such as the tension of the populace so frequently sets off. The presence of Annas and Caiaphas at this early hour was sufficient evidence of the source of the trouble.

Furthermore, Pilate had long since looked into the meaning of the word *Messiah* and this was not the first time that he had heard of this one. He had his own view of the subject. To him, the idea itself was outlandish, but messiahs certainly did not come within the scope of Roman laws. He believed, in fact, that it was the Jews' own fault if periodically some mystic proclaimed himself the Messiah. They never stopped talking of him or looking for his arrival. It was obvious that such a hope afforded a permanent temptation as much for impostors as for fanatics in good faith. Besides, by what signs was one to recognise the true Messiah? No specific test had ever been suggested to distinguish him from the doubtful or undesirable aspirants. In such a situation, how could the Jews avoid being made fools of whenever a simple soul or a clever opportunist, holding himself out as the Anointed of the Lord, took it upon himself to reprove the rich for their wealth or the priests for their frauds? With sudden indulgence, Pilate recalled the procedures attendant on the choice of a *flamen* or the installation of a *Pontifex Maximus*. Superstition against superstition, he definitely preferred those that were better systematised, leaving less scope to caprice, confusion, and petty quarrels.

He shrugged, listening with amusement to the more colorful parts of the report: the story of the ear slashed off by Simon Peter and restored by a miracle, the reference to the twelve legions of angels that, supposedly, the Messiah could call down from heaven in an instant. Pleased to encounter once more a folk lore that had become familiar to him since he took up his duties in Judea, Pilate felt his anxiety subside. He realised that there was no cause for unreasonable alarm. It was a routine matter that could undoubtedly be settled in a few minutes of talk with Annas and Caiaphas.

As to this, Pilate was deceiving himself. He was not a dedicated official. He was an optimist out of laziness, whereas it behooves the politician to be an optimist only by calculation—or rather to pretend to optimism in order to avert unnecessary difficulties before they arise or to try to expedite the solution of problems. With Pilate, optimism was not a tactic but the spontaneous consequence of his dread of complications.

In a passage outside the walls of the court and the offices, the Procurator, relaxed and almost casual, first greeted Annas, who had no official rank. Then, as if only just becoming aware of the presence of Caiaphas, Pilate murmured a polite platitude of greeting. This ranking, which gave Annas precedence, was intended to put the meeting on a more or less unofficial level: Pilate was receiving Annas, still a person of consequence although he had been deposed by Pilate's predecessor, and Annas had brought with him, no doubt by chance, his son-in-law, the president of the Sanhedrin. Neither Annas nor Caiaphas was deceived. At once they told Pilate the purpose of their visit, which, as he could imagine, was no mere courtesy call. The Sanhedrin, in plenary session, had condemned Jesus to death. The Seventy-One expected that the Roman authorities would confirm the sentence without delay. The formality was unquestionably required but it should take little time. That having been done, the Council would be obliged to the Procurator if he would carry out the crucifixion of the pretended Messiah during that day.

Pilate replied that there was no hurry. Then he asked whether the Seventy-One had really met, for it had been his impression that the group was called together only for the most important questions and this was obviously not in that category. And what dispatch! The arrest was only a few hours old; already sentence had been imposed and its execution was sought without delay.

Caiaphas explained the conditions under which the full membership of the Sanhedrin was required: matters concerning a tribe as a whole, the trial of a false prophet, the choice of a High Priest, a declaration of war, the expansion of Jerusalem, or a major change in the composition of the city. Jesus of Galilee was a false prophet. Therefore, it was the Seventy-One, not the penal section of the Grand Council, that must act. Its decision had been made: It was death. But assuredly the Procurator was not unaware that every death sentence had to be ratified by the occupying power. That was why Caiaphas, president of the Grand Council, had come to request confirmation. If his father-in-law, Annas, was with him, it was to demonstrate that he was lending his unanimously acknowledged prestige to support the judgment of the highest tribunal of the Jewish community, to which Rome had always granted the right to govern its internal affairs with complete independence and in conformance to its own legislation. But since Rome had reserved to herself exclusive discretion in capital cases, her representative must make the final decision on a sentence of death. True, the Grand Council would be unable to understand a reversal, which would contravene the judicial autonomy that had been solemnly accorded. Caiaphas requested, respectfully but firmly, the countersignature of the Procurator.

Pilate himself had proposed to the central administration this restriction, which, in his view, would enable him to restrain the excesses of fanatics. Today he was becoming acquainted with its drawbacks. In order to rid themselves of an agitator too popular for their taste, the Scribes and the Pharisees, under the pretext of respect for the law, were shifting the onus of his execution to the Roman authorities, whom the accused had in no way invoked. The chicanery with which he was threatened annoyed Pilate the more because it was his own innovation that had made it possible. He was determined to play a subtle game.

He had two arguments in reserve. In the first place, he could maintain that, contrary to the thesis of the Sanhedrin, the Procurator, being solely responsible for capital punishments, was in no way obliged to approve automatically every sentence imposed by the local authorities: It was his duty to initiate a new investigation, to render justice on the basis of its findings, and then to take the necessary steps for the execution of the sentence. Furthermore, he understood that the Messiah was a Galilean. In that case, he would normally fall within the jurisdiction of the courts of Herod, tetrarch of Galilee. Now, by good luck, it happened that Herod was at that moment in Jerusalem.

Consequently, not so much from conviction as to uphold the principle of the prerogatives of the Roman authorities, Pilate declared that he reserved the right to examine the charges made against the Prophet in the light of the laws that he was obliged to apply; but first it seemed to him proper as well as courteous to summon the prisoner before Herod, tetrarch of the state of which the accused was a native. This need take only a few hours, since Herod was in Jerusalem.

He rose to end the discussion. He knew, as the priests too knew, that Herod, son of a king who owed his crown to Roman support, and who besides was of Idumenian descent, would not willingly enter into a purely Jewish quarrel. Annas and Caiaphas attempted to object. Pilate interrupted them coldly: "What I have said is said." He left the place without even bidding them farewell.

An hour later, a message from the Sanhedrin was brought to him. The Council emphasised the fact that, by proclaiming himself "king of the Jews," the agitator struck directly at the sovereignty of Caesar. Hence, the matter had become as much political as religious and the Procurator himself was directly involved. Even if it were to be assumed that the Prophet had violated none of the laws of Rome—and this was by no means certain—Caesar's representative could not exonerate a usurper of power. If he took such a risk, he would be making a serious decision and the Sanhedrin would be compelled to transfer to him the entire responsibility as far as Rome was concerned. No doubt the Propraetor of Syria, whom Pilate was obliged to consult in important matters, would take a different, perhaps a more severe view of his duties.

The blackmail was blatant. This was not the first time that the priests had resorted to it. But this time the danger was clear. In the case of the shields, it was Vitellius through whom the Jews had submitted their appeal to Tiberius and it was Vitellius who had conveyed to Pilate the Emperor's abandonment of him. The position that would be adopted by the Propraetor of Syria in this new dispute was not difficult to foresee. Pilate congratulated himself for having thrown on Herod the onus of what promised to be a prickly matter.

In fact, however, Pilate was once more mistaking his desires for reality. It was true that the Galilean proclaimed himself king of the Jews and that Herod, normally, should be charged with suppressing him; but the tetrarch was too clever to compromise himself in a matter that concerned primarily Jews and Romans and in which straw monarchs, such as himself, could only lose. Herod acted quickly. Soon a guard of legionaries brought the Messiah to him, dressed in the white of the innocent. Innocent in both meanings of the word—having done no wrong and having lost reality.

Pilate had been informed that Herod had bidden the prisoner perform a miracle to prove his divinity; Jesus had kept silence. Pilate was disappointed at this frustration of his ruse. He thought it strange—but then, on reconsideration, very clever—to have asked the Prophet for a miracle. There was no more impressive way, it appeared, to strip a Messiah of his shams. And at once his memory repeated a scrap out of his youthful reading: ". . . God, who performs no miracles without reason and who owes none to anyone." Assuredly, the sophists had had an answer for everything. . .

Nonetheless, the Procurator was still resolved to resist the Sanhedrin. Jesus himself, obviously, meant little to him. From what Pilate had learned, he seemed a better man than his persecutors. He was hated by those whom Pilate most loathed—fanatics who would certainly never be swayed by the wisdom and tolerance of the Greek philosophers. If only to annoy the Sanhedrin, Pilate was tempted to simply set the preacher free. Unfortunately, the excitablility of the populace was such that the matter could hardly be hushed up. A quick solution was required. Passover had just begun; tomorrow would be the sabbath. Above all, the persistence of the priests disturbed him. Pilate had the presentiment that he was gambling his whole career, his safety. Vitellius, his superior in the chain of command, had the ear of Tiberius. Should there be trouble, he would be only too happy to blame the Procurator's conduct again; following the incidents concerning the banners, the aqueduct and the shields, it was bound to mean his recall. Even if nothing serious occurred, Vitellius would not forgo the opportunity to transmit and to endorse the complaints of the Grand Council. He would accuse Pilate of frivolity or negligence, or else of compounding his known mistakes through his abstract intellectual approach.

Exasperated, Pilate considered that he had been ambushed. At the same time, half in earnest, half in mockery, he regretted that such distasteful problems lacked even the compensation of taking his mind off his stomach troubles.

A slave broke in on his reflections with word that his wife wished to see him, and a centurion came to inform him that the crowds in the streets were growing larger and more agitated. They demanded the death of the Prophet, but for the moment they did no more than shout. The troops were having no difficulty in containing them, but the situation could explode in an instant. Pilate sought to account for the speed and the size of the demonstration. He suspected that it had been instigated by Annas and Caiaphas, but he was astonished at so disproportionate a reaction to what he considered his ingenuously deliberate, impartial, and equitable position.

He was not aware that he had refused the High Priest; no doubt, he had been somewhat dilatory. He had raised points of law, but they were altogether appropriate. He had let it be understood that the surrogate of the Emperor, however punctilious in cooperating with the local authorities and maintaining respect for law and order, could not blindly and automatically adopt their views. He might have added that the policy of the empire had to take into account some extremely complicated facts and that in the instant case he was not yet completely informed. These were the set speeches that he customarily used in analogous situations and that are familiar to most officials. He had not said this, probably because of a kind of unconscious deference to the experience and acumen of antagonists who undoubtedly knew what worth to place on such ritual phrases. And besides, what more could be expected of a high Roman official aware of his obligations? In short, Pilate was sincerely convinced that he had conducted himself with complete poise and that his opponents, as reasonable men, must have had to accept his arguments. After all, he was not their procurator merely to make them happy!

Actually, neither Annas nor Caiaphas had had the slightest illusion as to Pilate's inner attitude. They knew that he was inimical to them, but they had persuaded themselves that the Procurator's well known lack of moral courage, especially after his loss of face over the shields, would dictate an immediate surrender. They could not wait. Jesus was popular in the countryside, where everyone believed in his supernatural powers and where the priests had little influence. If the news of his arrest were to get abroad before the announcement of his execution, there was reason to fear that his disciples would enlist enough followers to liberate him by force. Hence, the majority of the Sanhedrin, on the basis of facts supplied by Caiaphas and advice furnished by Annas, had lost no time in forging the pincers for a double pressure on Pilate—the threat of denunciation to the Propraetor of Syria coupled with that of a popular uprising to compel the Roman governor to execute a treacherous rebel against Rome.

Pilate was just beginning to grasp the magnitude of the stratagem, without any clear insight into its motivations, when his wife was announced. Pilate loved her very much, but principally out of selfishness and his inability to do without her. When he had been posted to Judea, he had conditioned his acceptance on permission to take his wife with him. This was completely contrary to custom, if not to regulations. A special order from Tiberius had made it possible for Procula to accompany him.

She came in pale and distracted. She told her husband that she was harassed by a dream and that it was essential that he save the Innocent whose death the Jews demanded. The poor woman had chosen a bad time. This was hardly what Pilate expected of her— the aggravation of his troubles by her intervention in so stupid yet complicated a matter. And worse, it was not to advise him in a precarious crisis that she had come, but to tell him a dream. It was too much. Why should she worry about a dream? But Procula was extremely perturbed, and Pilate was as weak in his marriage as in his office. He resigned himself to listening to his wife's story and pretended interest. But out of vanity, as well as to emphasise his indulgence, he pretended also a certain impatience.

Procula's dream had taken her wandering in an underground maze peopled with furtive, feverish creatures. The walls were painted with fish and lambs that now and then came alive. Harried by the sound of heavy steps and the clinking of breastplates, she had the feeling that invisible soldiers were closing on her. The air grew thinner, the corridors multiplied, her faith in the Prophet became an inescapable duty to decipher the markings of the fish, the wool of the lambs, as if there were a meaning to be found in scales or curls. Procula knew that the fate of the Messiah depended on her, but she could not read the secrets of the fish and the lambs. She groaned that she could read only letters. A voice replied that she would be held responsible nonetheless for a frightful error from which the civilised world would suffer for centuries.

Pilate must exploit his power to prevent the tragic mistake. The Gods did not give such warnings twice. *Sunt geminae somni portae. . .* Through those double doors came dreams that forewarned as well as those that misled. But surely this time the oracle was not one of those fraudulent fantasies that the *Manes* send through the ivory door. Pilate must heed it and save the Messiah from a nefarious crime. Procula was still trembling, drenched in sweat.

Pilate wanted to answer that they had passed beyond the day when the magistrates of Rome were influenced by auspices or auguries or dreams, by the entrails of sacrificed animals or the hunger of the sacred fowl. But he took pity on his wife's wretchedness, and in spite of himself he was impressed by the fervor of her recital. He did his best to calm her, and he explained that dreams were equivocal and difficult to interpret, that they had a disturbing way of mingling useless emotions with the incoherent images of which they were composed and that it was essential that one refrain from ascribing specific meaning to an anxiety caused by winding passages, painted fish, and phantom soldiery. He promised, however, that he would ask an opinion on the meaning of the dream from his friend, Mardouk, who was a Chaldean and hence adept in the exegesis of visions.

Such a promise was not onerous. For one thing, Mardouk's conversation always charmed him, diverted him, and calmed him. For another, the characteristic of the Mesopotamian that Pilate most esteemed was a skepticism that exceeded his own, which he had long believed unique until he had met Mardouk. It would be a pleasure to spend a reassuring evening in Mardouk's villa. He would have an opportunity to amuse Mardouk by telling him Procula's dream. Mardouk would find some plausibly calming explanation. And that would be an end of it. In fact, Procula's tranquility was already almost restored by Pilate's mere promise, for the reputation of Chaldeans as interpreters of dreams was immeasurable. Leaving her husband, she asked him to forgive her for having been so importunate in the midst of his problems.

TWO

Menenius

PILATE
RETURNED TO SERIOUS
MATTERS. BUT HE HAD NOT
STOPPED PONDERING PROCULA'S
DREAM. HE BERATED HIMSELF
FOR HAVING ALLOWED
HIMSELF
TO BE BOTHERED BY
SUCH NONSENSE. BUT THE
AUTHORITY OF DREAMS
AND THEIR
MYSTERY IS SO GREAT THAT
EVEN THOSE MINDS MOST
ARMORED AGAINST THEM CANNOT
ESCAPE THEIR INFLUENCE.
HE DECIDED TO SUMMON THE
PREFECT OF THE PALACE
TO DISCUSS THE PROGRESS OF
EVENTS AND THE BEST
MEANS OF COPING
WITH THEM.

The centurion whom he ordered to fetch Menenius took advantage of the opportunity to tell Pilate that the sentries were finding it difficult to restrain an apparent lunatic who insisted on speaking to the Procurator in person. The man claimed to be a disciple of the Messiah and insisted it was he who had sold Jesus to the priests for thirty pieces of silver.

Pilate embraced the opportunity to question a man who could be so self-contradictory. It could give him valuable insights into the mentality of the sect. He resolved to see the man after he had consulted Menenius. Meanwhile, he would send word to Mardouk that he would call on him in the evening, after dinner, if that was agreeable to his friend. Then he called in the prefect and described the trap that he thought the Sanhedrin was trying to spring on him. The priests were trying to shift to him the disgrace of deliberately executing an innocent man whose only fault had probably been that of treating them as whited sepulchres. The figure was forceful but not unwelcome to Pilate, who found it felicitous. In any case, street demonstrations had been begun. Should he give in? It was certainly the simplest course, and it could cost only one man's life, whereas an uprising would bring about many more deaths. On the other hand, it was humiliating and undoubtedly in the long run dangerous for the power of Rome to bow before the first rabble of fanatics that came clamoring. Furthermore, the Messiah was worshipped by a great part of the country people. His execution by the legionaries would bring down on Rome only a new flood of hatred and—as far as the priests were concerned—in all likelihood not so much gratitude as a proof of weakness that would not be forgotten quickly. What did Menenius think—he was a knowledgeable, prudent politician, whose long years of service in outlying dominions had liberated him from pettifogging scrupulosity at the same time that he had ripened in valuable experience.

"Sire," Menenius replied, "we must get out of the situation as quickly as possible. The whole thing began badly. The trouble at the Mount of Olives was vexing enough. And it defies explanation. The Prophet taught in the Temple every day. It would have been simple to arrest him in broad daylight with complete conformity to the law. But instead of a normal arrest, there has been a kind of punitive expedition that in itself constitutes an attack on public order. Result: A servant of the High Priest lost an ear. The country is not too quiet. We are not very many; Rome saw no obligation to reinforce our garrisons. Let a revolt erupt and we shall not grow old in Judea. It would be better to yield, at least for the moment. We shall lose face temporarily, I grant, but it is the lesser evil.

"The safest course would be to execute the Galilean. Besides, if you let him go he would probably be torn to pieces by the mob. Even so, I agree that it is irritating that Rome should be involved. It is a question of getting out of the hornets' nest without seeming to take sides. I know: Jesus is innocent; or, rather, he is innocent from our point of view. To the priests he is guilty. That should be enough for us. They know this question better than we; it is their business. What is more, the order from Rome against becoming involved in local quarrels leaves little leeway to the discretion of the governors. True, the monopoly on death sentences entrusted to us at the same time does not ease the task. Well! it is not the first time isolated officials have had to puzzle a way out of contradictory orders.

"There are two errors to be avoided: one is placing Jesus under the protection of the Roman army;

the other is assuming the responsibility for his execution. I know the subtleties of these people here: it will
not be long after having demanded it of us that they
will be blaming us for his death. In the villages, the
poor believe in him as the Messiah which, furthermore, he says he is. The man is rather a demagogue,
even if he does seem innocent. In the end, innocent or
not makes little difference to us. For once I agree with
Caiaphas—not that I accept the argument that that
guttersnipe presents when he talks with you—but I
endorse the principle that underlies his policy. It is
more or less this: 'It is not undesirable that one man
die for the salvation of a people.' Or it has been put
this way: 'Better injustice than disorder.' It comes to
the same thing. This, it seems to me, is the inevitable
slogan of any policy worthy of the name. Once we
accept it, we must consider the consequences. . . To
govern is to look ahead, is it not? Now, it would be a
piece of remarkable stupidity not to make sure that
we avoid being called torturers and murderers by the
very men who are now putting pressure on us to give
them their victim. It should be quite clear that he is
their victim, not a martyr in the struggle against our
occupation. Let us not lose sight of the fact that, whatever their internal rivalries, to all of them we are still
the hated oppressors. No change of heart is so un-

likely that we can afford not to be prepared for it.

"Here is my suggestion. Time is pressing. It is now the moment for practical measures. Today is a holy day on which, according to tradition, a prisoner is given amnesty. Let the mob choose between Jesus and a robber I have in a cell; his name is Barrabas. You can be sure the crowd will choose the thief. First of all, the Sanhedrin will see to it. And then, too, a criminal does not excite the passions as a prophet does. The mob will choose Barrabas in order that Jesus be crucified. Then, let the thief go, as if reluctantly, and make it clear that this is not your choice. Let them know that you are bowing to tradition by releasing the prisoner they choose and that you wash your hands of the other man's death. I am not speaking figuratively: it is essential that you wash your hands on the balcony, really in public. In all Judea, and far beyond as well, this is the ritual gesture to save oneself from the stain entailed by evil-doing or sacrilege, to forestall the consequences of a threatening dream or a bad omen, to advise the soul of him who has died by violence that it must seek its rightful vengeance elsewhere. Everyone will understand. Trust my experience. This magic is the rule. And washing one's hands takes on symbolic meaning so naturally that there is no danger of looking ridiculous to the central administration.

"I will see to it that a pitcher, a basin, and a towel are at hand at the tribunal of Gabbatha. I myself, when it is time, will pour the water over your hands.

"One more word of advice, if you permit me, Sire. Have the Prophet crucified with common criminals so that the execution seems less political and it is not obvious that Rome is yielding to the pressure of the Grand Council. Similarly, it will be advisable not to disclose the burial place of the Galilean. The tombs of rabbis are honored here; they are places of pilgrimage and hence of meetings."

Pilate was puzzled. He admired the shrewdness of the suggested solution. But for the first time, very definitely, he was ashamed of being a man to whom anyone would cold bloodedly, as a salutary step, dare to propose a crime. Completely unexpectedly, the chief result of Menenius' speech had been to show Pilate suddenly that to permit the execution of Jesus, when he was in a position to prevent it, was no less a crime than to kill him in cold blood. Until now, Pilate had not thought of this. It was personal dislike of Annas and Caiaphas rather than respect for abstract justice that had made him refuse their demand. He had not even imagined the argument that Menenius had just presented to him as being the basis for the thinking of Caiaphas. Certainly, for an administrator, injustice causes less embarrassment than does disorder. But to proceed from that to the view that it is to be preferred. . .

Now, even though he knew so well the exigencies of government, he was shocked by a formula that, nonetheless, he had employed all his life from habit, from inertia, without regret, as if mechanically. The brutality of the concept made its meaning unacceptable to him. Why was it necessary to put things so crassly? It was as if the painful duties of government were rigidified in absolute rules of conduct. "Of course," he told himself once more, "injustice is preferable to disorder." He knew how the theme was developed, of course. What did it matter if by a stroke of bad luck some tainted blood was shed? The welfare of all justifies the sacrifice of one. But why should this injustice be made as it were official, why give it the aura of wisdom, the prestige of idealism? Pilate could act, had acted according to these rules. But he disapproved of them and he was revolted when they were quoted to him.

Menenius, who had frequently observed a similar

reaction in the Procurator, did not hesitate to characterise it openly as both immaterial and hypocritical. Pilate could say nothing in reply except that he still felt that the frank statement of such principles and their acceptance with complacent resignation, perhaps only pretended, could only lend them cogency, exaggerate them and taint man's conscience at the root. The Roman would have sworn that Jesus of Nazareth proclaimed exactly opposite principles, outrageous in the eyes of men of politics. Was it right, however, to sacrifice a great number of people in order to save one just man?

His head swirled with vertigo but at the same time he sensed in these paradoxes of principle a link with the lessons of his Stoic teachers, a kind of projection of them. In principle, Pilate agreed that justice should be done though the heavens fell, but he could see no way of reconciling that precept with the duties of a governor. Nothing was more to be desired, in his eyes, than the approval of a Cato weighing the judgment of the gods with a heart of wisdom. This was not for him, who dreaded displeasing the Propraetor of Syria, much less the Emperor.

Pilate knew he was weak but at the same time justice had for him a stubborn fascination that he lacked the strength to refine into an active passion. Once again, undoubtedly, and not without some self-contempt, he would take the easy way.

"Find a pitcher and basin of pure silver, then," he told the Prefect, "and a spotlessly white towel. At least, if the act itself is dirty, let the instruments be elegant and the symbolism beyond reproach."

He was joking, but the essence of his irony cut through the rhetoric and was less frivolous than it might appear. The gratification of duty done, of the disinterested rendition of justice, of a generous impulse that does not waste away in sterile thought but is translated into action: this satisfaction is fragile, dubious, costly. The reward rarely matches the sacrifice. The latter, therefore, maintains its value, and its rarity as well. Everyone loses heart and little by little acquires a more cautious, more selfish outlook. Within oneself one permits the corruption of a firmness that one can never regain. One continues, however, to feel the need for it. Some turn then to art or some other external aspiration to find a substitute. They look for the equivalent of the purity, the perfection, the absolute that had first attracted them in a more intimate, more demanding realm. They contemplate themselves forever pursuing a similar ideal in a sealed-off world, immune to shocks, to dangers, to bewilderments, where it is no longer necessary to dedicate oneself or to pay with one's soul. Such a course generally seems the fruit of wisdom and experience, but the heart is not deceived. It recognises the irrevocable renunciation. The mind and the emotions can now savor exquisite pleasures, which have indeed their own nobility and which are in fact the flower of every civilisation. They make it easier to forget many things; not all, not memory, not the regret for a vital loss suffered in that moment when the basic, ineradicable sense of human solidarity was as it were repudiated in favor of the love of art or of some other rich indulgence. Pilate was aware of this.

He remembered the madman in the custody of the guard and went to question him.

THREE

Judas

THE MAN SPRANG UP. HE WAS
FLUSHED AND GAUNT.
HIS TORN AND FILTHY ROBE, HIS
EXCITEMENT, HIS JERKY
MOVEMENTS HARDLY ELICITED
SYMPATHY. PILATE WAS
SORRY THAT HE HAD COME AND ALL
BUT ORDERED THE MAN THROWN
OUT WITHOUT A HEARING. THEN
HE CHANGED HIS MIND. AS
LONG AS HE HAD COME
DOWN . . .
ABOVE ALL, HE DID NOT
WANT THE LEGIONARIES
TO SENSE THAT HE REPENTED
HAVING GIVEN HIMSELF
THE TROUBLE TO LISTEN TO
SOME WRETCH. ONE OF
THE SOURCES OF PILATE'S
WEAKNESS WAS HIS CONCERN WITH
WHAT OTHERS THOUGHT.

"I must enlighten you, Procurator. You are ignorant. You do not know the Holy Scriptures; I do. You have not reflected upon them. How could you understand their meaning? Even the most zealous of the Savior's disciples do not understand what must be done. My name, which will be execrated for centuries upon centuries, means nothing to you: It is the name of a tramp picked up by your police. It is also that of an instrument of Divine Providence. Through my ministry, everything shall be accomplished; through mine and through yours, Pontius Pilate, Procurator of Judea. We have lodged in the same inn, embarked on the same galley. But you do not know it yet, Procurator. Hence, your whim or your concern with justice can incur the risk of ruining everything and leaving all the nations of the earth doomed to eternal damnation. For you, I know, can save the Messiah, rescue Him from execution, because He is innocent. Like that fool, Simon Peter, who raised his sword last night to defend Him. But He knows what He does.

That is why He bade that simpleton sheathe his sword and why He restored Malchus' ear. He knows.

"It was I who pointed out the Savior to Caiaphas' men and who had Him arrested in the night like a criminal, like a conspirator, like an agitator, when the whole city had just spread a carpet of palms under the hoofs of his donkey and when all of them, at last beginning to open their eyes, were kissing His hand and recognising in Him the Son of God. It was difficult for me. I had to convince the priests and the captain of the guard, I had to pretend I wanted money and ask for thirty pieces of silver so that they could understand my treachery as the product of greed. It was the best motive to claim, with such greedy men. But I do not want their money; the moment the so-called betrayal succeeded I threw it in their faces. I asked for it only to make them believe me and take the necessary action: an arrest that would create a stir and that they could not undo, that would make it impossible to suppress the news or treat it like an insignificant misdemeanor. Insignificant! The salvation of the world depends on the crucifixion of Christ. If He lives, if He dies of old age, or of the bite of a horned viper, or of the plague, or of gangrene, or whatever, like anyone else, there can be no Redemption. But thanks to Judas Iscariot and to you, Procu-

rator, that will not be the case. The Son of Man, as
he is called, will be crucified publicly and his bones
will be counted. The veil of the Temple will be
ripped from top to bottom and darkness will cover
the earth at midday. God dies for the salvation of man.
He redeems both the Jews, who hate Him, and the
Romans, who know nothing of Him; and their children and their children's children. Each drop of his
blood redeems each one of them. Like you, Procurator, I am the minister of the Divine Sacrifice.

"No matter that you do not understand. It is
enough that you give the order today to crucify Jesus,
as Caiaphas demands, and the world will be saved by
the self-sacrifice of the Son of God. Do you know
that no less than the martyrdom of God's Son can
save man? It will be said that you were a coward and
I was a traitor. What weight can that have against
what is at stake? I am not an informer, I am not a
traitor. I, like you, carry out the Divine Will. It is
the will of Jesus that you have Him crucified. He
will not even answer your questions. It was with love
that He pointed out my part and my privilege at the
Supper last night. The others despised me at once;
they looked at me with disgust. Those criminals,
those blasphemers wanted to prevent the Master's
execution and thus destroy the meaning, the great-

ness, the infiniteness of his renunciation. But I understood. I handed over the Master as if He were a thief in the night, and you, Procurator, will have Him crucified. Do not make any great-hearted gesture; do not destroy the Redemption of Man by releasing the blameless One I have betrayed. Fulfill the Scriptures and assure the glory of the Savior through the very shame of his tortures. You must understand that death on the cross will guarantee the Divine Message. It will be the authenticating seal and signature. We are the necessary artisans of the Redemption, He said: 'Evil must be done, but woe to them that do the evil.' We are the agents of the supreme evil, who will make God suffer in the flesh of man and die the death of a slave for the salvation of His creatures.

"I had to tell you this because I do not trust your cowardice. It is impossible ever to be sure of the cowardice of the most cowardly. I was afraid of some sudden surge of courage in you. I preferred to tell you everything. Farewell; it is done. There is nothing left for me but to hang myself. Perhaps you will hang yourself too, Procurator, when children point their fingers at you and you are a target of universal disgust because you washed your hands of His blood. From this day our two names shall be joined through all eternity: the Coward and the Traitor. In reality, the

Bravest and the Most Faithful—the one whose weakness was so necessary, the other so devoted that he is willing, for love, to be marked forever with the stain of crime. You will be cursed, but console yourself. He knows that He could not have redeemed man without my feigned treachery and your false cowardice. Accept, as I do, the sacrifice that will give us precedence over the greatest of the saints."

A sudden epilepsy interrupted his raving. He rolled on the ground, foam at his lips. Pilate, with a gesture, ordered that the revolting spectacle be removed from his presence. But he was trying to discover some meaning in the shocking harangue.

He did not succeed. The whole tirade seemed nothing but delirium. How did these people attain such grotesque stupidity? What sense could be made by the idea of a God who died for the salvation of man? In the first place, a God does not die; it would be a contradiction. In the second place, a God does not concern himself with the fate of humanity. That would be ridiculous. And to imagine that a Roman magistrate should be available expressly to fulfill some ancient Jewish prophecy was really insane. "So insane," Pilate said to himself, "that I must tell Mardouk about it this evening." The thing really should be clarified. The Roman, indeed, expected not a really rational explanation so much as an intelligent discussion of beliefs of the messianic sects, a picture that would make it possible for him to form some idea of the important and more or less providential part that the fanatic had ascribed to Pilate in the indispensable execution of his God. No one could guide him through the maze of these gibbering superstitions so well as the Chaldean.

Mardouk's ancestors, natives of Ur, had established themselves in Palestine some generations earlier. Mardouk had inherited a modest estate outside the city near the cave called Jeremiah's, on the way to Caesarea. Situated among quarries and cemeteries, the property produced dates, olives, and figs. The Chaldean was an enthusiastic student of sects, doctrines, and rituals. He looked for their interrelations, examined their differences, and regarded their antagonisms and their similarities as a kind of geometry, at once delicate and vast, that provided him with great pleasure. He would say with a smile, but it was easy to see that he was not altogether joking, that he knew of only two exact sciences: mathematics and theology. The latter, he would add, accorded the more with his own taste.

His father had named him Mordecai, in honor of

the old Biblical character, the son of Yaïr the son of
Shimeï the son of Qish, of the tribe of Benjamin,
whom Haman had sought to destroy with all his people. But Mordecai's niece, Esther, having asked a hearing from Ahasuerus and succeeded in persuading
him, had miraculously won his mercy for her uncle
and all their people when everything seemed hope-
less. An annual holiday still commemorated the occasion. The new Mordecai's studies had led to him to
identify his namesake with the ancient god, Mardouk,
and Esther with the goddess, Ishtar. From this he had
derived an audacious commentary on an especially
sacrosanct chapter of the Holy Book. But he had kept
to himself the secret of discoveries that he had every
reason to believe it dangerous to publish. However, in
subtle recognition of his own daring and very plausible thesis, he had changed his name of Mordecai for
that of the old god. Hence he was known under the
puzzling name of Mardouk.

On several occasions, he had had to request the
permission of the Roman authorities for journeys into
some remote or dangerous area populated by ad-
herents of an exotic cult. Since an escort was necessary, he had been referred to Pilate, who had thus
come to know this distant forerunner of the science
of ethnography. A warm friendship had grown be-

tween them, no doubt originating in the skepticism that was common to both but varying in each. Pilate viewed religions as so many unreasonable superstitions devoid of interest. Mardouk was interested in nothing else, believing that they could teach more about human nature than could any other source, especially the abstractions of philosophy. Pilate respected this point of view without sharing it; in any case, he found it restful and pleasurable, particularly in contrast to the narrow pedantry of the learned men of the Temple. In anticipation, he was already enjoying the clarifications that his friend would offer on the ravings of a traitor bedazzled by his own treason.

FOUR

The Interrogation

LOUDER AND LOUDER, THE VOICES
OF AN ANGRY MOB APPROACHED.
MENENIUS CAME TO TELL
PILATE THAT THE LEADERS OF
THE SANHEDRIN HAD
GATHERED
OUTSIDE THE PALACE, WITH
THEIR GALILEAN PRISONER, AND
WERE REQUESTING THAT
PILATE GO OUT AND QUESTION
HIM IN THEIR PRESENCE. HE
REFUSED POINT-BLANK. HE WAS
TIRED OF YIELDING TO
EVERY CAPRICE OF THE PRIESTS.
"LET THEM COME IN IF
THEY LIKE OR STAY OUTSIDE
IF THEY PREFER." HE HIMSELF,
CONFORMABLY TO ROMAN
PROCEDURE, WOULD CONDUCT
HIS INVESTIGATION
IN HIS OFFICE

He ordered the soldiers to bring in this Prophet, the source of so much irritation. The Nazarene was led before him, still wearing the white robe that Herod had ordered put on him.

"Are you the king of the Jews?" the Procurator asked.

"Do you say that I am," Jesus answered, "or have others told you so?"

Pilate considered the distinction meaningless and remarked to himself that it was he, not the prisoner, who was asking the questions. He replied:

"Am I a Jew that I should answer you? Your people and their priests have brought you before me. What have you done?"

"My kingdom is not of this world. If my kingdom were of this world, my soldiers would have fought to prevent my being delivered to the Jews. But my kingdom is not here."

"Then you are a king?"

"It is you who say it. I am a king. I was born for

one thing, for which I came into the world: to give testimony for the truth. Whoever is for the truth will listen to me."

Pilate could not help smiling. The truth? How simple! And how ingenuous to speak of it with such assurance! Truly, an illiterate, the son of some unknown workman, born in a forgotten village, could hardly understand the inextricable complications that surrounded such a concept the moment one tried to analyse it. The Roman recalled the controversies of the sophists and the Greek polemics. He was at once touched and vexed.

"What is truth?" he asked, aware of the futility of the question but using it as a kind of test.

Jesus did not reply.

"You say your kingdom is not here and you came into the world. From where?"

Jesus did not reply.

"You do not wish to speak to me," Pilate said. "Do you not know that I have the power to set you free or to have you crucified?"

"You would have no power over me if it were not given to you from On High. Therefore, the fault of him who delivered me to you is the greater."

Pilate recognised that the man was constantly referring to some *beyond* on which he believed the real world depended. There was no sense trying to follow him along this line. He would end this ridiculous interview; one does not contradict the deranged. He went outside and spoke to the leaders of the Sanhedrin:

"I can find no guilt in this man. No more could Herod, since he sent him away."

The rest of his thought was this: "He lets it be said that he is the king of the Jews and at the same time he contends that his kingdom is not of this world. It is a contradiction that proves only that he is out of his mind. He said also that he was the Son of God. That means nothing—we are all the sons of the gods. He is presumptuous, speaking of truth as if he knew what it was. But there is nothing to do but let him talk. As far as I am concerned, he is harmless; according to my information, he even advises the payment of taxes. Rome asks no more."

The mob muttered. Caiaphas was stunned. He had never thought Pilate would take so definite a stand. He had been aware of the Procurator's resistance earlier that morning. But he thought he knew him well enough to believe it would not last. The Roman was casual, tolerant, and supercilious. He hated having to inflict punishment or take decisions, especially in matters that bored or annoyed him and that, besides, were delicate and might well evoke criticism from Caesar. Furthermore, the dispute over the shields reminded him that it was not easy to disregard the clearly expressed desires of the Jewish authorities.

If Pilate was so reserved, it was unquestionably because he did not recognise the seriousness of the situation. To be sure, in the excitement aroused by Jesus he saw not a dangerous assault on a religion and a clergy toward which he did not hide his indifference, if not antipathy, but a healthy agitation, common among the devout and the superstitious and at the same time a welcome escape vent for political passions and nationalistic grievances. Because they were confident of Pilate's tendency to view the matter in this perspective, and still more because of the Procurator's well-known horror of complications, Caiaphas, Annas, and all their friends had convinced themselves that Pilate would give them a free hand at the first opportunity, delighted at not having to take a position.

They were crushed by Pilate's public and categorical declaration of the innocence of Jesus. It was so unforeseen that for a moment they almost considered it a miracle and believed in the claimed supernatural powers of the impostor. In addition, their surprise made them overestimate the import of the

Procurator's statement, which was not the pronouncement of a judge, delivered from the tribunal and having the force of a judgment, but a mere personal opinion lacking legal force. They were so bewildered at Pilate's seeming assumption of responsibilities that he could have evaded that their fear became panic. They saw the power of Rome protecting a sacrilegious vagrant who blasphemed against the Holy Faith and openly insulted its priests. That a Roman patrician should despise the Jews was to be expected, but it was no reason for a responsible official to side with the rabble against the best element. Romans or Jews, priests were priests—guardians of the framework of society and servants of the gods. There was no question of asking a Roman to worship the true God, but it was not too much to ask of a magistrate that he respect priesthood wherever he encountered it. Pilate must certainly not have realised that he had just lightly and more or less capriciously thrown over the political and religious leaders of the nation for the sake of an agitator from the dregs of the populace, who relied on the mob and stirred up slaves and harlots. This was tantamount to dissolving the solidarity on which every society was necessarily based. Besides, given the man's character, it was completely incomprehensible. Why was Pilate defying them?

They were frightening themselves for nothing. For Pilate, preoccupied as he might be with Stoic justice, was primarily concerned with the interests of Rome and had by no means forgot that, if things went wrong, he still had as his last resort the pitcher, the bowl, and the towel that he had ordered Menenius to prepare. But Caiaphas thought in his apprehensiveness that he must strike hard and fast. He cried:

"Whoever calls himself king declares against Caesar. If you release Jesus you are disloyal to Caesar."

The threat was direct and unequivocal. Behind the priests, the demonstrators they had stirred up shouted that the Prophet must be crucified. Pilate was frightened, but he was equally afraid to seem in their eyes to be yielding to so bald a blackmail.

"I have no intention of releasing Jesus. He will be punished as he deserves. Tomorrow, before my tribunal at Gabbatha, as is the custom, I will give you the choice between him and Barrabas. For the present, I shall show how Rome deals with his pretended majesty."

The crowd shouted that it chose Barrabas and that Jesus must be crucified at once. But at the same time it was titillated by the prospect of the promised spectacle. Pilate, meanwhile, was giving orders to Menenius: concentrate combat troops around the palace, throw a wall of legionaries, three ranks deep, between the mob and the buildings, avoid bloodshed for the moment but kill if necessary.

Then he told the soldiers to dress the prisoner as king of the Saturnalia and flog him as they pleased. They cloaked him in a purple robe and wove a crown of thorns that they forced down on his forehead. Into his hand they put a long reed, the travesty of a scepter. They whipped him with the customary wooden rods and with whips of hide tipped with bits of bone and lead weights. They bowed mockingly before him, saying: "Hail, king of the Jews." Then, rising, they slapped him and spat in his face.

The opened gates allowed the mob to miss nothing of a scene that delighted it but revolted Pilate. Nonetheless, he congratulated himself on the flash of inspiration that had begot this clever trick: to make of the king whom he was reproached for tolerating a joke like the mock king who was crowned in Rome on the Kalends of January. Perhaps—at least, according to Mardouk—the feast of Purim, which the Jews celebrated on the 14th and 15th of their month Adar, derived from the Babylonians, who also flogged and then crucified or hanged a false king to whom sovereignty had been transferred for five days at the beginning of spring. In such case, the meaning of the scene would not be lost on the crowd.

At the same time, Pilate hoped that the cruelty of the spectacle would arouse some pity in the demonstrators, or at least act as a kind of appetiser of torture that would stay their hunger for the main dish —that is, the crucifixion. Above all, keeping in mind the threat of Caiaphas, the Procurator felt confident now that he could dispose entirely of the contention that he accepted an impostor who claimed to be king of the Jews in Caesar's place. A majestic king, this masquerade monarch degraded under a storm of taunts and blows. Pilate thought too that it would not hurt the madman to endure a little rough handling that would bring him back to reality.

He had Jesus taken outside in his ludicrous costume of crown and robe and reed scepter. The rabble mocked and laughed. This apparent good humor, which was nothing but savagery, convinced Pilate that he had dominated the situation. He called for silence and said: "Here is your man." He believed the mob would be satisfied with the sight of Jesus in so grotesquely pitiable a condition. But the demonstrators shouted: "Crucify him! Crucify him!"

"Shall I crucify your king?" he jested. To crucify this rag of a man, who had to be held upright, seemed out of the question. He felt he had done enough.

To make it clear that he had not been taken in and that, in his view, the matter would remain unresolved until the actual execution of the prisoner, Caiaphas answered solemnly: "We have no king but Caesar."

"Tomorrow, at the tribunal of Gabbatha," the Prosecutor replied.

The security guards were now at their posts. Pilate went back into the palace and sent the Galilean to a cell. Without, the crowd was still shouting, trying to break the guards' ranks. The Procurator had a short meeting with Menenius, who was strongly critical of his having refused to end the affair then and there by surrendering Jesus. Then he went to his quarters to sleep until it was time to go to Mardouk, tell him what had happened during the day and enjoy his unfailingly instructive and amusing analysis; if the occasion arose, to ask his counsel. After this endless day, so rich in events at once bewildering and annoying, Pilate needed such an interval, which would be far more refreshing than the troubled sleep that he would endure during the heat of the afternoon.

FIVE

Mardouk

AT DUSK,
PILATE ORDERED A
LITTER AND SET OUT FOR
MARDOUK'S VILLA. JERUSALEM
WAS QUIET.
SUN AND HEAT,
WEARINESS AND HUNGER
HAD ERODED THE ANGER OF
THE POPULACE. BUT THIS
WAS ONLY
A TEMPORARY RESPITE;
THE PROCURATOR WAS
NOT UNAWARE OF THAT.
FOR THE MOMENT, THE
EVENING WAS COOL AND
PROMISED A PLEASANT NIGHT.
THE FIRST STARS SHONE
IN THE DARK BLUE SKY.
THE NIGHT-BLOOMING CEREUS
WERE OPENING, THE
HIBISCUS
WERE CLOSING.

This simple, unchangeable procedure filled Pilate's spirit with a feeling of peace that he rarely enjoyed. He took pleasure in imagining the succession of various flowers and tried to identify them as each scent came to him.

He was already in the garden and the predominant odors were those of the flowers that Mardouk's servants grew. Mardouk himself was waiting for Pilate at the portico of his house. Under the breeze, the leaves of the date trees stirred like great tired spiders. A peacock was sleeping in the dark. On a low table, almonds so fresh that their feathery rinds crackled between one's teeth had taken the place of the red cored fruits that Lucullus used to have shipped to Rome and that Mardouk, in their season, liked to provide for his guests.

When they had greeted each other, Mardouk gestured to a servant. The man drew a large dark object from a nearby well. "I have followed the poet's advice," the Chaldean said:

"The goat-skin bottle keeps the white wine fresh,"

and he went on, jokingly:

"Oil-colored lemons, cold water to the taste,
Hang with the flowers from the twisted trees."

He motioned toward his trees, in support of the quotation, and ordered the flagons filled. A firefly glowed in the deepening shadows.

Pilate told of the arrest of the Prophet and the conversation with Annas and Caiaphas; confident that he was speaking to a man convinced, he accused them of bad faith without mincing words. He repeated the suggestions of Menenius and recounted his questioning of the prisoner and what had followed; then, as a kind of diversion, he told of Procula's dream. Finally, as fully as his recollection permitted, he repeated the strange harangue of the maniac who had come to persuade Pilate to join forces with him in order to accomplish the Scriptures by having the Redeemer crucified.

What redemption had he in mind? Had Mardouk ever heard of these weird ideas? Were they widespread? Were there really sects that believed that a king of the Jews, the Son of God, must die on the cross? Mardouk knew the Procurator's good faith, he could be sure that Pilate would never make any political use—still less police use—of anything Mardouk told him.

Mardouk reassured him. He held Pilate in great regard and knew that in such matters he was characterised by a discretion that was completely incompatible with his duties. It occurred to him that Rome must in fact place small importance on Judea if she sent out a governor in whom disinterested love of knowledge was so prominent a trait. As to the facts of that day, Pilate's story, though rather inaccurate, did not greatly surprise him.

"Your prophet must be an Essene," he said. "Do you know about the Essenes?"

Pilate knew nothing of the Essenes, the Sadducees, the Shebans, any more than he suspected that the peacock sleeping in a corner of the terrace was venerated as the Spirit of Evil and the Prince of this World in peaceful villages along the Tigris and Euphrates. His tutors had made him read Plato and Homer.

Mardouk explained who the Essenes were. They looked forward to the coming of a Lord of Justice whose reign would bring about a deep and decisive transformation of the hearts of men. They forbade the use of violence and taught universal brotherhood. "If a man strike thee on the left cheek," they preached, "offer him the right." They believed in the immortality of the soul and emphasised that the primary rule of life was to love one's neighbor as oneself for the sake of the Lord.

It was completely night. There were many fireflies now, darting and diving and soaring in their phosphorescent ballet. The servants had brought torches of vanilla-scented resin; they filled the flagons whenever they were empty.

"There will be neither masters nor slaves," Mardouk continued. "That is what they prophesy. If their predictions, which are merely their desires, are realised, relations among men will be forever altered. As you know, I spend my time studying religions. I am quite serious when I tell you that theirs is the best and, if I did not believe in all faiths at once, I should request the baptism that is the ritual for joining their congregation. I swear to you, Procurator, that, if this religion triumphs, time will no longer be counted from the founding of Rome but from the birth of the Lord of Justice. And rightly so, I think, for that date will have marked an event of more significance than the foundation of a capital."

Pilate accepted the impertinence without a flicker of an eyelid. The wine had already induced a certain detachment of mind. And, in this garden, it was a point of honor to forget, and to make his host forget, that he represented the power of Rome. Besides, when he was younger, he had been fascinated by the legends of the Etruscans, which set a term to the lives of cities and empires as if they were men, and which foretold the exact date of the fall of Rome. His eyes followed the flashing dance of the fireflies.

Mardouk himself was somewhat swayed by the wine, by the course of the conversation, and by the strange attitude of acceptance that he sensed in his companion. He began to elaborate on the eventual results of the triumph of the new doctrine, its spread among the poor, the anxieties of the authorities, the inevitable persecutions, the courage of the martyrs, the aristocrats seduced in their turn, as if infected by an inescapable epidemic, ultimately the conversion of the Emperor and then the counterattack of the old faiths, their futile resistance, their slow disappearance. To make his words more dramatic and more convincing, he began to describe the catacombs. Suddenly he had the explanation of Procula's dream. He told of the hunted lives of the believers and spoke the Greek word for *fish*, which represented in their proper order the initials of the words in the same language for *Jesus Christ, the Son of God, the Savior.*

Then, in contrast, Mardouk spoke of the Blemmyes, who led a savage life in southern Egypt and had obtained a treaty with Rome that authorised them to take the statue of Isis worshipped on the island of Philae and carry it off to the inaccessible rocks of their kingdom. After a few months, they would bring it back to its sanctuary with great pomp. The triumph of the new religion would not change this tradition for a long time, Mardouk explained, and the last priests of the pagans, as they would then be called, would be able to maintain a forbidden worship through the fear inspired by their savage tribe. Finally, after the massacre of the Blemmyes by the Nubians, the Bishop of Smyrna would take possession of the island, root out the old religion and scatter its priests afar, ending the terror of a life behind their temple walls, threatened daily by a new fanaticism and lightened only twice a year by the departure of one set of guards and the arrival of new ones with cargoes of ritual offerings, presented with affected piety by grinning warriors with painted faces and filed teeth.

Mardouk felt as if he were conjuring, inventing credible suppositions. But his imagination was less active than he thought. It was the opposite of what happens in a dream, when the sleeper dreams he is reading, in a nonexistent book, a passage that actually he creates as he goes. The dreamer believes the text has been given to him and that he merely takes cognisance of it, reading from line to line and turning the pages. For Mardouk, the contrary was true. He was convinced that he was imagining everything, shaping it with his knowledge and his intelligence. But, in fact, it was all irresistibly filling his mind without his playing any part. He did not deduce or assume or infer. He only became aware of a vast invisible panorama that offered itself without his perceiving the fact.

Everything of the future—all the possibilities of history—came to him at once, as fugitive, as thin as the fleeting flashes of the fireflies, glowing and vanishing like a rapid script erased as soon as written. Such a text could never have been set down; still less could it have had anything to do with even an unimaginable alphabet or any coherent system of meaningful symbols. So Mardouk deciphered the evasive, the evanescent history of the world, or at least one of the infinite potentials of that history.

Mardouk told of Herod and Herodias dethroned and exiled to the frigid Pyrenees at the other end of the world, the Pillars of Hercules, in Lugdunum Convenarum, which would come to be called St. Bertrand de Comminges—for cities and towns would be named for those who had died to advance the new religion or for bishops famed for their piety. Out of tact, he said nothing of Pilate himself, whom he saw unseated by Vitellius, recalled to Rome, then exiled and finally killing himself in despair in Vienne in Gaul after the death of Tiberius. Nor did he speak of the canonisation of Pilate by the Coptic Church, for which the nineteenth of June would be designated in the calendar as the day of Pilate and his wife, Procula—Abroqla, in the harsh tongue of Abyssinia—honoring her for her dream, him for his ineffectual scrupulosity, his futile efforts, and his attestation to the innocence of the Redeemer. Long afterward, a harsh French or Scottish cleric would pronounce this sanctification monstrous.

Mardouk preferred to explain the problems that would swarm round the new pastors; he listed the heresies, the councils, the schisms; he described the rivalry of the temporal powers, the struggles between popes and kings, who would again call themselves emperors. He pictured the birth and the conquering drive of other religions, the battles of Poitiers and Lepanto, the swift Mongol horses before Kiev, Cracow, and Vienna on the Danube. With satisfaction and skill, he created a possible future, peopling it with as many names as possible because he had observed that the most improbable fantasies were easily accepted as soon as they were authenticated, as it were, with family names, dates, exact locations, statistics, references to registers, and diaries. Mardouk knew enough languages and was sufficiently astute in the laws of phonetics and philology to give credibility to the names he forged, despite their sometimes disconcerting sound. He pretended to pronounce with great difficulty the syllables of tongues still to be born, and yet he was somewhat surprised each time to find them as if already developed and offered to his use.

The flashing emerald sparks of the fireflies went on weaving patterns in the dark as Mardouk described the artistic masterpieces that would be brought into being by unparalleled inspiration: the porches of Reims and Chartres, the Irish illuminated manuscripts and the Coptic tapestries, the pictures in the brothels of Abyssinia recreating the meeting of Solomon and the Queen of Sheba—so many and so marvelous that he could not attempt to name them all or describe them. He imagined (or professed to imagine) the discovery of a New World and the manifold incidents attendant on its conquest—the ships deliberately set afire, the tree of the love of Malinche, and the victory of Cortez. In his desire to luxuriate to the utmost in the riches at his disposal, he mingled out of all order the triumphs of art and the agonies of history. Further confusion arose from the fact that he was seeing everything at once and would suddenly remark that he had forgot to mention a vital fact or an important episode. And, in addition, his natural preference led him to accent the extraordinary and the disturbing.

He anticipated the fate of Byzantium and described the marbles of St. Sophia, the symmetrical veins of which would portray devils and camels. He summoned up the entry of the Crusaders into Constantinople (Byzantium was to change its name), then the capture of the city by the Turks; and then, returning to the arts and leaping over several centuries, Delacroix' painting of the Crusaders' entry into the city, Baudelaire's verses in praise of the picture, and the critical applause for Baudelaire's verses. Time was a transparent mass in which he traced one series of ideas after another in a kind of intoxication.

Mardouk wanted to demonstrate how all things were interconnected even to the least of details and how an immeasurable manyness of events could be found contained by implication in a single invisible seed: the choice of road at a vital fork. But who could know in advance which direction would be the determinant? Let Pilate beware! Perhaps he would arrive at one of those mysterious crossroads at which, careless or inattentive, he would be the blind agent who for centuries diverted the fate of all mankind. As an extra proof, Mardouk invented (or thought he was inventing) the names of future theologians who would devote learned dissertations to Procula's dream; he enumerated the dreary list of these monographs, with the dates and places of their publication—Gotter's, published in Jena in 1704; Johan Daniel Kluge's, in Halle in 1720; Herbart's, in Oldenburg in 1735 (all dates of the future epoch). He even found an acceptable name for the French writer who, a little less than two thousand years later, would reconstruct his discourse for publication by Gallimard and Macmillan—and no doubt he flattered himself that he had imagined that name.

Pilate listened while he drank and followed the flight of the erratic insect glows as if to find in it some indecipherable signal. He was amused and grateful. He let himself go in the unexpected pleasure of this game that in other circumstances he would have found asinine. He enjoyed hearing a clever mind imagine the whole history of the world, not as prophecy but as free, if rational, deduction; it was a connoisseur's delight. Pilate congratulated himself for having thought of visiting Mardouk that evening to get away from his worries. The pleasure of the evening exceeded his hopes. Worn out with his fanatics and his visionaries, he was grateful to his host for playing the prophet without claiming to be one and for offering a fiction so rich in details: names of kings and philosophers, of rivers and fruits, all seeming so natural as soon as heard. Mardouk seemed to be composing his anticipatory history as a poet fashions an epic, bringing in new episodes or polishing old ones to give the whole a greater coherence. These artistic subtleties, these expert appraisals exercised a flexible, vigilant supervision over an exquisite fancy. Such virtuosity was exactly what Pilate needed to distract him from the burdens of his office.

Pilate's eyes had not left the green insects. Coming suddenly into view, they rose almost vertically until they could not be seen. Then they came down, gradually reappearing, glowing only when they were almost at ground level. It was as if the earth were constantly shooting new ones aloft in a continuous eruption. But it was always the same fireflies that flew back and forth, leaving their wakes of burning emerald in the shadows. Between two invisible boundaries the lines of light crossed and recrossed and diverged and came together in an allegory of the gentleness and the extravagance of nature, a symbol of Mardouk's talk, a cluster of living sparks and a refreshment for the mind. Altogether at peace, Pilate surrendered himself to a double and parallel vertigo: the darting of the fireflies and the fanciful evocations of the Chaldean.

An unexpected turn of the conversation brought it back to the remarkable beliefs that had been its starting point. Mardouk was telling of the meeting of a Slavic novelist with a gymnosophist on the banks of the Ganges, the result of which was to be the restoration of India's independence. After long subjection, that country, in which Alexander had sought to establish Macedonian domination, would regain its freedom through a movement conducted by the ascetic and forbidding violence on principle. Thus the doctrine of the Essenes, which might have been thought ludicrously unsophisticated, might not be devoid of political force. Undoubtedly, it was a necessary condition that the force against which this deliberate weakness was arrayed be fearful and cautious, doubtful of its own morality. But was that not, from now on, the case with the force at Pilate's command, the brutal and systematic use of which revolted him? Why otherwise did he hesitate to crucify the Galilean, as the priests and the mob demanded? Had it occurred to the Procurator, from another point of view, that the martyr's glory is often essential to the victory of a Prophet? It was in this light that Mardouk under-

stood the otherwise incomprehensible plea to Pilate
by Judas. That fanatic was so passionately dedicated
to the teachings of love and sacrifice as expounded
by his Master that, to assure the triumph of his faith,
he would have used his own hands to assassinate the
man he believed to be the Messiah. There was logic in
his attitude; except that assassination would not be
enough because it is almost always born of passion or
vengeance, gain or madness.

An execution ordered by a court was preferable
—a formal punishment imposed by the decision of an
appropriate judge in conformance with law. Thus
the violence would be an official act, its injustice
would be unarguable and the process of cause and
effect would be set in motion without interruption
or delay. The sacrifice of a Messiah could never seem
an accident, compared with the death of a philosopher
who, like Socrates, chose to die in order to obey the
laws of a city of men. An incompatibility of quite a
different kind must be made apparent: that between
divine charity and political order. That was why, all
things considered, Mardouk wondered whether it was
not advisable that tomorrow the Procurator should
adopt the course urged by the madman, who, on
second thought, had shown himself an intelligent and
persuasive disciple. In this fashion, Pilate would make

his own contribution, simply by taking no action (and, true, at the cost of an innocent man's life), to bringing on the new order. The reward made it worth while; and the professed Redeemer, after all, had run a tremendous risk in exposing himself not to crucifixion but to exoneration.

Pilate rose. He was pale. Neither man was drunk, but both had suddenly lost their detachment and that first pleasant euphoria that comes from good wine and the free play of ideas. The fireflies had abandoned their games. The Procurator shivered, as if he felt the coolness of the night. In fact, his inner eye had glimpsed, in the place of the dancing insects, the pitcher, the basin, and the white napkin.

"I think," he said, "that neither Socrates nor Lucretius would have thought highly of a religion that relied on injustice or a man's cowardice to lay its foundation."

Mardouk was constrained, unable to guess what he had said that could have got under the skin of a man whom he believed—in this respect, at least—detached and unemotional. But, accompanying Pilate to his litter, Mardouk was vanquished by his insatiable desire for the last word:

"That only proves that neither Socrates nor Lucretius nor you have a religious soul. In their hearts, neither Socrates nor Lucretius thought highly, as you put it, of any religion."

Mardouk was thoughtful when the Procurator had gone. Rejected names and visions still crowded his mind. He saw long lines of men in rags plodding slowly along mountain paths, through rocks and underbrush. They marched in compact groups, each far behind its predecessor. They held one another by the hand, the elbow, the shoulder. They were constantly going off the path. When one of them fell, the guide of the group tried to put him back on his feet, often without success. Sometimes the guide would shove back into the mass a man who had wandered away and, suddenly aware of his aloneness, grasped wildly at the air.

They were the fifteen thousand Bulgarians captured by Basil II the Younger, the emperor whom the panegyrists lauded as the Equal of the Apostles. He had ordered the prisoners' eyes gouged out and then sent the men to Tsar Samuel. In each group of a hundred there was a man who had been allowed to retain one eye: he guided the ninety-nine blind. When they reached the distant capital and when the gruesome parade of the fifteen thousand, long since reduced in number, passed before Samuel, he swooned in horror, to die insane two days later.

Mardouk would not allow himself to envisage other atrocities, though many blurred pictures tried to enter his mind. He drew back from the slaughters and massacres of the future that crowded on his thoughts. He shrugged, as if to shake off the nightmare. He was beginning to doubt. He wondered whether, lecturing Pilate, he had not over-estimated the capacity of religion to civilise men's hearts. Then he rejected the doubts: if faith in an All-Powerful, who was at the same time All-Loving, could not influence man to master himself, what other instrument was there? Of course, Mardouk admired the wisdom of Lucretius and even more that of Socrates. But was it wise to rely on wisdom to change the world? Wisdom, by its nature too reasonable, seemed to the Chaldean neither evangelical nor contagious enough. On the other hand, faith, as dangerous as it was . . .

Mardouk stopped short. He was talking without thinking—he, who knew so well that he was a man of thought, not of emotion. Why must his own astuteness make him think fanaticism, blindness perhaps, was more fruitful?

SIX

Pilate

PILATE WAS DISCOURAGED AND
PERPLEXED. MARDOUK'S BARELY
DISGUISED ADVICE DISTURBED
HIM. HE WAS STUNNED BY THE
CULMINATION OF A LINE OF
REASONING THAT HE HAD
FOLLOWED ONLY IN A KIND OF
REVERIE. HOWEVER DIFFERENTLY
INSPIRED, IT COINCIDED IN PRACTICE
WITH THE POLITICALLY
MOTIVATED SUGGESTION OF
MENENIUS AND THE RAVING
EXHORTATION OF JUDAS. BUT IT
WAS THE DUTY OF MENENIUS TO
PROVIDE RESPECTABLE CLOAKS
FOR CYNICAL SOLUTIONS: AND, AS
FOR JUDAS, IT WAS OUT OF THE
QUESTION THAT A MAN OF
COMMON SENSE SHOULD PAY
ANY ATTENTION TO THE
DELIRIUM OF A MANIAC.

By contrast, Pilate had always given the greatest consideration to Mardouk's deliberations.

In that outpost of the world where almost everything was alien to Pilate and where the spirit of the people accorded so little with his own, Mardouk was the only man whose conversation he enjoyed and in whom he could confide with some hope of enlightenment and guidance. Though Mardouk was his junior, Pilate looked on him as an elder, a master whose thinking was sharper and deeper and whose experience and knowledge surpassed his own. Mardouk, without knowing it, was Pilate's outer conscience. And now he was joining, or seemed to be joining, in the unnatural coalition of the politician and the lunatic, standing surety for momentary expedients and unrestrained fury. And finally he took their side immediately after having once more demonstrated, in a magnificent improvisation, the wealth of his talent, the superiority of his cultivation, that originality that endowed every paradox with evidentiary authority—

in short, what Pilate was sometimes tempted to call his genius.

Perhaps Mardouk wanted to test—or tempt—him. Pilate sensed that this was close to the truth. But he had still to determine what the Chaldean had sought to test in him; Pilate was sure that it bore no relation to feelings of honor or respect for justice. The materialistic reasoning of Menenius had not held Mardouk's attention for an instant. On the other hand, he had immediately explained the motivations that made the behavior of the talkative Jew intelligible. He had almost admitted their solid foundation. Now Pilate thought he knew the answer: Mardouk had stirred him up in order to discover whether something in Pilate could understand or conceive other aspirations, recognise, or feel other needs than the laws of moderation, of reason, and of equity so arduously evolved by mankind through centuries of groping and of error, laws whose total victory over so many powerful instincts, over the very sap of life, man would probably never succeed in establishing.

Mardouk had wanted to convey to him the thought that the force of the immoderate was necessary to strengthen the desire for moderation, that reason required something of madness in order to claim the right to impose its own kingdom and that the primitive violence of universal injustice was the sole source of the strength that could hasten the uncertain advent of a precarious and approximate equity.

Pilate felt reassured and at the same time somehow cheated. He gloried in his loyalty to a purely human system. Adoration of gods was not his strong point; nor was faith, credulity, superstition, any submission to mysterious powers whether animal or supernatural. Man's salvation, he believed, lay only in man himself. That was why it upset him that Mardouk, who believed no more than he in the existence of gods, urged him to act as if they existed. What he overlooked was that Mardouk, though he might not believe in gods, accepted that drive in men that made them incessantly invent gods. That was the difference.

In any case, taking metaphysical sides could in no way help the Procurator, who would wake next morning to face the same hard decision. Like every Roman of his class, Pilate had studied law and entered public life because tradition had it so. His successes had been sparse. His taste for Greek philosophy made him contemptuous of a profession that to him seemed beneath a man of wisdom. He longed to be able to strive in solitude toward some ideal of personal perfection, but he lacked the courage to resign his post. It held him by its routine, its substantial material advantages, and

the pride he felt in telling himself from time to time
that his duties gave him almost unlimited power over
a great many lives.

He practiced an imaginary Stoicism. He valued
nothing so highly as strength of mind and impregnable
objectivity. He took pleasure in imagining himself
looking on without a tremor at the disintegration of
the universe, demonstrating under the most difficult
conditions an unbroken serenity invulnerable to temptation and threat. Success did not unsettle him and
no disaster could wound him. Naturally, he had ac-
quired no reputation. His innate indifference to the
responsibilities of his position had made him a medi-
ocre, if conscientious, functionary. To be at his age
a mere procurator at the perimeter of the Empire was
hardly brilliant, especially for the descendant of Pontius Cominius, who, in 387, when Rome was besieged
by the Gauls, ran the Tiber on a raft to rally the de-
fenders' courage with news of the victory of Camillus.
But Pilate derived no pride from this ancestry, or from
his connection with Pontius Telesinus, whose head
was paraded on a spear round the ramparts of Praeneste
at Sulla's orders to frighten the troops of Marius, or
from his kinship with Lucius Pontius Aquila, one of
the plotters who stabbed Julius Caesar on the Ides of
March.

Pilate was not unhappy over his mediocrity. He lived obscurely, forgot in his remote outpost. Though he lacked ambition, he would have liked a transfer to another province, for he found the Jews hard to endure. He had arrived well disposed toward them, amicable from policy as well as from weakness. It had taken little time for their religious intolerance to repel him. All strange beliefs were possible—in a sense, even normal, what was to be expected of the human race, still shrouded in the shadows of savagery. Nonetheless, there were limits. Stupidity did not establish the right of stubbornness even if it prevented fanatics from seeing the virtues of others. Whenever Pilate had tried to convert the chief priests, most of them Pharisees, to what he considered a humane and reasonable outlook, he had aroused more anger and hatred than if, instead of trying to convince, he had simply commanded. Hence, trapped by his own gambit, by having vitiated his authority with his own suggestion of a discussion, he had most often yielded, but each surrender left more bitterness that endured, like the dregs of a poison. From time to time, however, he had tried to be firm and succeeded only in acquiring a name for cruelty.

Not long after his arrival he had caused the legions to march through Jerusalem with unfurled banners.

Above the eagles they bore the portrait of the Emperor. This portrayal of a human face was a sacrilege to the Jews; hitherto, the Romans, respecting their beliefs, had always left their banners at the city gates. The next day, a delegation had gone to Caesarea to request the withdrawal of the portraits. For seven days they entreated Pilate. Then he ordered the emissaries to return to their homes. When they refused, he threatened them with death, and the legionaries drew their swords. The Jews declared they were ready to die for their faith. Impressed, Pilate retreated and agreed to remove the banners.

In another case, he had expropriated funds from the treasury of the Temple to pay for the construction of an aqueduct. When he came to Jerusalem, the Jews attacked his residence. The Procurator sent the legionaries into action. Several men were killed and many were wounded. Nevertheless, Pilate had gone ahead with the aqueduct, for to him it was ridiculous not to divert to the welfare of the community a treasure that would otherwise have lain fallow. Then, only recently, there had been the matter of the shields, when the Jews complained to Vitellius and Tiberius so humiliatingly disowned Pilate.

Each time he had attempted to act for the best; each time his cowardice or the occasional brutality that takes the place of energy in the weak had been unlucky for him. He had come to despise himself. He was ashamed, far more on behalf of the philosophy he professed than for the sake of the authority for which he was obligated to maintain respect. He could not pretend that it was not his spirit rather than Rome that was defeated each time he gave ground. Each defection pulled him back still farther from that ideal of reasoned firmness that he had paradoxically established. Occasionally he burst out and abruptly imposed a decision. He derived no inner profit from this, quite convinced that he owed the victory to fear of the legionaries or to the prestige of Caesar rather than to his own qualities. Another man might have considered it normal; Pilate was mortified by it. This man of fifty, for whom physical pleasures were growing more infrequent and more banal, found less and less opportunity for that self-esteem that is the major consolation of those who feel the vigor of life diminishing.

Sometimes Pilate saw himself as the victim of an insidious and implacable fate. The lack of a strong, unchanging direction in his ordinary behavior allowed his slightest derelictions to feed on one another and endowed the most trivial, which were naturally the most numerous, with a fearful pressure of inertia.

Weakness, chosen at every opportunity, became second nature, and the Procurator could foresee the time when, his back against the last wall, he would no longer have the strength to combat the feeblest obstacle. The reasons why men say *no* had long since lost their primal urgency for him, so that he despaired of his capacity for even the slightest resistance. He forgot that, to counter the acquiescence that was slowly eroding his courage, there existed in him as in every man a mysterious reserve of hidden strength, like a bed of ancient rock concealed by shifting soil. A series of accidents, rapidly becoming something else, had made him vacillate and fear. But another force, subterranean, inherited, timeless, formed of an infinitely greater number of favorable circumstances, hard choices, heroic refusals, imposed its own weight and its own inertia, which in turn sustained a secret penitence in a Roman procurator debased by his own impotence. The pupil of rigorously clear thinkers, he could not avoid suffering from each of his surrenders, and he could not forget them. His memory, his heart harbored a passion that, dormant at present, could explode tomorrow.

Meanwhile Pilate rendered unto Caesar that which was Caesar's, which, for the sake of comfort, he reckoned to be little. Barricaded behind a book of rules, or the prudence of the politician, he let the world go its own way as much as possible, without intervening in what did not concern a procurator and often scorning what a more devoted procurator would have looked into. He preferred to investigate abstract problems that fed his fantasies rather than his intellect. As often happens, the defect of his character had spread to his intelligence: he found more pleasure in futile speculations and unintelligible subtleties than in problems that called for sharp and simple solutions.

This time Pilate was caught. No postponement was possible. Tomorrow he must either let Jesus die or, to save him, sacrifice his own comfort and his career—accept a host of problems, stand firm against both Jews and Romans: against the priests, who would bitterly resent his resistance, and against his subordinates and the propraetor and their condemnation of a decision that would be not only ridiculous but dangerous. As usual, he unleashed his imagination, already seeing himself a kind of hero battling them all—the insistence of Annas and Caiaphas, the plea of Judas, the advice of Menenius, the bait of Mardouk—to surrender himself nobly to the daggers of the fanatics who would certainly never forgive him for having protected the blasphemer.

The thought excited him but, also as usual, gave

him no courage. These dream heroics did not seduce him; on the contrary, they strengthened his conviction that he was always the one to give in, to take the easier way. He was tired of being the man who washed his hands. That was why, earlier, he had responded so smartly to the stimulus of the Chaldean.

What Mardouk had counseled was, in truth, something quite different: the deliberate sacrifice of his dignity, of his concept of justice, of his considerable vanity, for a cause far superior to his wretched self. But Pilate knew too well that, for him, the delivery of the Prophet to the priests would be not a painful sacrifice freely accepted but a cowardly escape, one more of his abdications.

SEVEN

Night Without Sleep

BEFORE
GOING TO SLEEP,
PILATE DECIDED
TO ANALYSE THE
SITUATION AGAIN, COLDLY,
OBJECTIVELY, TREATING HIS
PERSONAL
INVOLVEMENT
ABSTRACTLY. IF, AFTER ALL,
THE EXECUTION OF THE
PROPHET
WAS DEMONSTRABLY
THE BEST SOLUTION, HE
WOULD HAVE NO REASON
TO REJECT IT ON THE
PRETEXT
THAT IT HAPPENED
ALSO TO BE THE EASIEST
AND MOST COMFORTABLE
COURSE FOR
HIMSELF.

Similarly, if a merchant seeking a state contract surreptitiously gave money to the purchasing officer to persuade the latter to buy his goods, the official would unquestionably be guilty of accepting a bribe, but it did not necessarily follow that the resulting transaction would not be the most beneficial for the public treasury. Other factors counted for more.

Now it appeared to Pilate that he had exaggerated the threats to his career posed by the release of Jesus. In any case, the Jews always found occasions to denounce his administration, as did Vitellius to file critical reports on it. Furthermore, the case in hand was only a petty one, which Pilate would explain in his own way, and he would be believed. In anticipation he answered the accusations that Caiaphas would make if he went to the propraetor of Syria. The most serious charge—that Pilate had allowed the madman to claim to be king of the Jews—was negated by Pilate's having made a mockery of his kingship. It was true that some of the Galilean's doctrines could be viewed as subversive of morality, of public order, and of government of any kind. But Pilate knew many philosophers whose teachings were notoriously more dangerous: to name only one, there was Diogenes.

Pilate had been told that, in this connection, Caiaphas had made a major issue of the driving of the money-changers from the Temple and of the pardon granted to an adulteress. Undoubtedly, both incidents were the result of deplorable thinking, but the one was not likely to end business or the other to endanger the fidelity of virtuous wives. Furthermore, Pilate considered that merchants did not belong in houses of worship; and he recalled having enjoyed the caresses of more than one lady of Rome whom he should have been angry to see stoned for her consideration. A much more serious question was that of military obligation, the refusal of which might well be a consequence of the Messiah's teaching. But was military service expected of Jews or other conquered peoples? It would be eminently unwise; at times even suicidal. Then there was the question whether Romans in the mass would espouse the new religion. This hypothesis was most unlikely, despite Mardouk's amusing inventions. Pilate was in no way capable of looking so far ahead to possible trouble, and his character was not such as to try. It would be time to consider the risk when it became unmistakable. But there would have to be answers, at least on the political level, to the unavoidable requests from Rome for an explanation.

Besides, the liberation of the Prophet would probably set off a rebellion. But he had enough soldiers to suppress it. He did not believe in the possibility of widespread or long-drawn-out struggle. Even the quarrel with Annas and Caiaphas would soon lose its edge and things would go on as before: a reciprocal antagonism barely concealed by formal politeness. Thus the Procurator would be incurring little risk by protecting an innocent man.

But to set the Messiah free was still a gamble. Anxiety again took hold of Pilate: suppose he was wrong? suppose the mob began to loot and burn (Oriental mobs ran amok in a moment)? suppose it overwhelmed the legionaries? Menenius was right—there were not enough combat troops to withstand a revolt of any real consequence. Already Pilate saw the Romans compelled to give up Judea. Had he the right to take that chance?

In contrast, crucifying Jesus would guarantee peace. But it was a crime. What statesman did not commit crimes, was not constrained to commit them for the public good? No government could function if one deferred to such paralysing scruples. No one could deny that whoever wields power cannot keep his hands clean.

Clean hands! Luckily, he could resort to actually washing his hands before the multitude. Everyone would know they were not stained with innocent blood. He imagined again, this time without apprehension, the ingenious spectacle proposed by Menenius. He saw himself erect on a platform, proclaiming the prisoner's innocence and handing him over to his executioners; then the prefect approaching, pouring water over his hands outstretched above the bowl. Then he would dry them slowly, meticulously, with solemnity and deprecation. The most stupid could not help understanding that Rome (and Pilate himself) had no connection with the act of cruelty that would follow. As Menenius had forecast, the ritualistic performance would dazzle the popular imagination. Rome stood for order and justice. Everyone would clearly see and long remember exactly where hate, fanaticism, and savagery flourished.

Calm now, he turned over, in the hope of soon falling asleep. But, before he could sleep, he realised that he must discard a solution whose hypocrisy was suddenly unbearable: he would be acknowledging even more, ratifying and approving a crime and allow-ing the criminals to commit it. Of course, his intentions would be good when he stressed that, in his view, the condemned man was innocent and did not deserve to be put to death. His theatrical gesture would be carried through only in order to place the responsibility unmistakably. But what of his own responsibility when, in a position to prevent a murder, he knowingly encouraged the killers to commit it, saying: "Do what you intended, provided you understand that I do not approve"?

Was it really enough to shrug and turn away in disgust? After all, that was exactly what they asked of him. There was also the danger that guardians of the public order, basing themselves on his example as a precedent, might again find plausible reasons for remaining aloof whenever they found it to their advantage, on the pretext that thus a neutral observer could determine under the best conditions where right and wrong lay.

Ceaselessly Pilate attacked this same redoubt, whose very simplicity made it impregnable. On the one hand, the interests of the state; on the other, the evidence that he, Pilate, would be personally, deeply guilty if he allowed an innocent man to die, whatever convincing reason he evolved to justify his abstention. Then he decided once and for all to save the

Galilean. He forbade himself to reconsider. The question was clear, and he congratulated himself that at last he could sleep, since he had no more conflict and his conscience was at rest.

In an instant, he was again in agony. Now the mad logic of the informer and the analysis of the Chaldean assaulted his memory. He pictured himself as the indispensable secret instrument of the God announced by the Messiah. In the feverish impetuosity of insomnia he accepted and exaggerated the absurd superstitions of cults and the dizzy paradoxes of philosophies. Already he was reasoning half mechanically. His acquiescence in the death of the Prophet became sacred, essential, ordained through all eternity by a Higher Will that, in its heaven, relied on his lack of courage. The shameful death of a God that his selfishness made possible would bring Redemption to the human race.

And not only to the human race. A God could not restrict the benison of redemption to the inhabitants of the earth. He must likewise redeem the many races that, according to the Pythagoreans or perhaps Demetrius of Lampsacus, had lived on the uncountable planets since the beginning of time, their histories synchronised with and identical to that of men in the smallest details. At dawn tomorrow, on each of the stars scattered across the infinite sky, the same events would be enacted as on earth. Countless Pontius Pilates would wash their hands in public in order that countless Messiahs of brotherhood, already seized by patrols in the pay of identical High Priests after having been betrayed by identical traitors, be simultaneously executed on innumerable interchangeable crosses. And then, in the void of the air, there would begin on each planet the unalterable sequence of thousands and thousands of events conjured by Mardouk, which no Pilate had the right to prevent.

. . . Neither the right nor, for that matter, the power. For, in his haste and his half-sleep, Pilate slipped from one metaphysic to another and discovered suddenly that his act had been determined at the beginning of time by the eternal cascade of the atoms, in which he denied with swift passion that the subtle *clinamen* could effect the slightest variation. Not only would the crucifixion be repeated in space but, since the number of atoms and hence of their possible combinations was finite, the crucifixion of the Savior would be repeated without a foreseeable end throughout an inexhaustible perpetual cycle.

Pilate felt as if he had awakened. He was covered with sweat. The doubled limitless mesh of crosses bearing tortured gods vanished suddenly and Pilate was alone. He wondered whether he had been dreaming or whether a fever had sent him into a delirium of arguments that were not only mad but contradictory. It amazed him now that he could have so completely adopted and, as it were, manipulated the impossible lunacies that only a moment earlier had most repelled him. This was not the first time, moreover, that he had observed that dreams tended to seize on thoughts and feelings rejected during wakefulness, whether to afford them a fleeting if dramatic revenge or to exorcise their poison.

Hence Pilate felt no disproportionate self-reproach, even though he had not been quite asleep, for having been seduced by so many sterile syllogisms into regarding himself as the secret accomplice of his glorious victim and at the same time almost as the real victim of a cosmic determination: he, a loyal if not a dedicated official, he the Just whom the gods made forfeit to the accomplishment of some mysterious plan that did not even concern him. He was as if intoxicated by so remarkable a fate and, like the morning's madman, he was filled with indescribable happiness at the thought that shame and dishonor would be heaped on him, the model of the Just or at least of the Obedient.

He recalled the end of the evening with Mardouk,

when he had insisted that Socrates and Lucretius would have rejected a religion that based its growth and its triumph on a man's cowardice. True, this argument had not shaken the Chaldean. Now Pilate was beginning to perceive why.

All at once it was as if he had awakened again. His theological phantasmagoria collapsed like so much painted cloth. Now Pilate remembered the excitement with which he had been carried away long ago when he read the philosophy of Xenodotos, popularised by Cicero in his *De finibus potentiae deorum.* The title alone had bewitched him: *The Limits of the Power of the Gods.* According to the philosopher, no gods, no stars, no cosmic laws, not inflexible Fate herself could force the just man to an act that his conscience forbade. His consent was required. Wrongful acts were inevitably the result of ignorance or of pressure. Most of the time, furthermore, they were the daughters of Greed, which was blindness and pressure combined. When the soul chose evil, it did so of its own volition, tipping the scale by reason of the weight it shifted. Neither Zeus, seeking in vain to save Sarpedon from death, nor anonymous and implacable Fate had the power to force the soul to be weak or wicked. The power of the Gods ended where the aspirations of virtue began. Whatever the magnitude of the stakes

—even the salvation of the world—the human soul did evil only by its own desire. It was its own master. No omnipotence could prevail against its unique power of choice. Pilate found pleasure in the thought that, even if the God of the Jews, or any other, had discounted his weakness, he had the choice of strength.

There was, however, more flattery than comfort in the thought. He wished desperately that all had already been irremediably accomplished. He envied the Spanish conqueror described by Mardouk, who had deliberately burned the fleet intended to assure his retreat. He wanted to be at the outcome of his choice, to be able to say *All is done*, and to have to face only external problems: a riot, the treachery of Caiaphas, the reproaches of Rome. He was suffering from the freedom to take or not to take the fatal step. He thought he had seen clearly what his duty was, but he dreaded increasingly the hidden yet crushing mortgage accumulated by the tally of his previous failures. In his impatience, he was fascinated by the victory over himself that offered itself. Thus it is that at times one throws oneself upon the obstacle that almost everything in oneself still hopes to avoid. Perhaps Pilate had sufficiently tortured himself to cause his weakness to react thenceforth in the opposite direction. His suffering had not been useless. Attracted, exalted, dazzled by the courageous course, he felt now as if he were falling instead of rising.

He heard a groan from the next room. His wife must be having another nightmare; he decided that he would go in and waken her if he heard her moan again. The thought reinforced his returning peace of mind. Nothing is more reassuring than the knowledge that one can give reassurance. Pilate felt less alone, and went to sleep.

Epilogue

MENENIUS
WAS STUNNED NEXT
MORNING WHEN PILATE FORBADE
HIM TO HAVE PITCHER, BOWL,
AND TOWEL IN READINESS
AT GABBATHA.
ON THE CONTRARY,
PILATE GAVE HIM EXTREMELY
DETAILED ORDERS
TO DISPOSE AND
USE THE COHORTS AVAILABLE
IN SUCH A WAY AS TO MAKE
AN IMPRESSIVE SHOW OF A
FORCE THAT WAS ACTUALLY NOT
SO GREAT. FROM THE ROSTRUM
ABOVE THE SURGING MOB,
PILATE DECLARED JESUS
GUILTLESS, SET HIM FREE AND
PLEDGED HIS PROTECTION BY
THE LEGIONARIES AS LONG
AS MIGHT BE NECESSARY.

Rioting followed and once more, as was the custom, there were several deaths and many injuries.

Caiaphas complained to Vitellius and the propraetor stripped Pilate of his office in the year 788 of Rome. Tiberius died before the accused arrived in the capital to offer his defense. Pilate lost his case and was exiled to Vienne, in Gaul, where he did indeed kill himself—not in despair, as Mardouk had rather rashly surmised in the logic enforced by his vision, but quite happily, because a Stoic was always free to abandon life when he deemed the time propitious. Loss of office and exile would undoubtedly have come about in the same fashion if the Procurator had crucified Jesus, for Caiaphas and Vitellius, both of whom loathed him, were determined to destroy him by any means.

When the exoneration of Jesus became known there was widespread rejoicing among the Prophet's disciples. They had believed him doomed; and he was restored to them, his innocence proclaimed by Caesar's own representative. It was an almost miraculous triumph of right. For once, the powerful sided with the just and the persecuted. Very soon, however, Pilate's action began to be a disadvantage to the Rabbi.

Perhaps the more impassioned among the faithful remembered having spread the rumor that archangels armed with flaming swords would descend to deliver him from the cross itself. The archangels had lost their chance. Assuredly the disciples were not sorry that their Master had not been crucified. Nevertheless, they felt that his rescue by the heavenly hosts would have been more awesome than the ruling of an official. At times, it was as if they were disappointed that the Son of God owed his life to the rectitude of a Roman magistrate. It seemed out of keeping with his divine character.

Meanwhile, the Messiah carried on his preaching successfully and died at a great age. He enjoyed a great reputation for sanctity and for a long time pilgrimages were made to his grave. All the same, because of a man who despite every hindrance succeeded in being brave, there was no Christianity. Except for Pilate's exile and suicide, none of the events predicted by Mardouk came to pass and history, save on this one point, took another course.

Studies in Religion and Culture